Village Phone Replication Manual

Creating Sustainable Access to Affordable Telecommunications for the Rural Poor

by **David Keogh and Tim Wood**

United Nations

United Nations **Information** and **Communication Technologies** Task Force

Grameen Foundation USA

International Finance Corporation
World Bank Group

CGAP

infoDev

Copyright © 2005 United Nations ICT Task Force

The views expressed in this book are those of their individual authors and do not necessarily reflect the views or positions of the United Nations ICT Task Force, the United Nations itself, any of its organs or agencies, nor of any other organizations or institutions mentioned or discussed in this book, including the organizations to which the authors are affiliated.

Published by
The United Nations Information and Communication Technologies Task Force
One United Nations Plaza
New York, NY 10017

unicttaskforce@un.org

DEDICATIONS

This publication is dedicated to Village Phone Operators and their communities worldwide.

ACKNOWLEDGEMENTS

Grameen Foundation USA acknowledges the generous support of:

- Academy for Educational Development (AED)
- Consultative Group to Assist the Poorest (CGAP)
- The Grameen Bank
- GrameenPhone
- Grameen Telecom
- Grameen Technology Fund
- infoDev
- International Finance Corporation (IFC)
- Susan and Craig McCaw Foundation
- MTN Uganda
- The management and staff of MTN villagePhone
- Omidyar Network
- Iqbal Quadir
- United Nations Information and Communication Technologies Task Force
- USAID dotORG Initiative
- Professor Muhammad Yunus

We would also like to thank the United Nations Information and Communication Technologies Task Force Secretariat, located within the Department of Economic and Social Affairs of the United Nations, and Ms. Enrica Murmura who provided invaluable support to make this publication a reality. Additional thanks go to Ms. Anna Gedda and Mr. Robert de Jesus who assisted with the copy-editing, design and layout of this book, and to the United Nations Graphic Design Unit for the cover design.

ABOUT GRAMEEN FOUNDATION USA

Grameen Foundation USA works in partnership with the Grameen Bank, pioneer of small loans to the poor, to fight poverty all over the world. The Grameen Bank started in Bangladesh in 1976 as an action-research project that attempted to provide tiny loans to very poor people to allow them to start "micro-businesses." Twenty-eight years later, Grameen Bank has 3.96 million borrowers, 96% of whom are women, and has loaned more than $4.57 billion in amounts averaging less than $200. Grameen Foundation USA, a 501c3 organization, was established in 1997 to provide financing, technical assistance and technology support to the growing numbers of grassroots institutions that are successfully replicating Grameen Bank's success in countries as diverse as Malaysia, India, Uganda, Mexico and the United States. The mission of Grameen Foundation USA is to empower the world's poorest people to lift themselves out of poverty with dignity through access to financial services and to information.

The Grameen Technology Center is an initiative of Grameen Foundation USA, working to eliminate poverty by leveraging the power of microfinance coupled with information and communication technology. The Grameen Technology Center focuses on technology that:

- makes the delivery of microfinance services even more efficient
- enhances income generating opportunities for the rural poor
- provides poor communities access to information for better health and education.

ABOUT UNITED NATIONS ICT TASK FORCE

The Task Force was established by Secretary-General Kofi Annan to help identify ways to harness the potential of ICT for economic and social development by promoting partnerships of public, private, non-profit and civil society stakeholders to advance the global effort to bridge the digital divide.

As a global forum for placing ICT at the service of development, the ICT Task Force has grown in stature and influence since its inauguration in 2001. With the potential of ICT to enable the attainment of internationally agreed development goals becoming widely embraced, the Task Force provides a platform to discuss international norms, policies and practices through the work of its networks, working groups and members. The Task Force is not an operational, implementing or funding agency but provides a platform and focal point for discussing global ICT-for-development (ICT4D) agenda, including issues related to strategic direction, policy coherence and coordination and advocacy in relation to the global ICT4D agenda. It has the mandate to help forge a strategic partnership between the United Nations system (UNS), private industry and other relevant stakeholders in putting ICT at the service of development. Meetings, in particular a series of global forums focused on key issues held over the last two years, bring together Task Force members with international development and ICT experts, policy makers, leading private sector representatives and members of civil society and non-governmental organizations and provide a platform for sharing experiences, exchanging views, catalyzing new partnerships and building consensus in complex and politically sensitive policy areas.

ABOUT CGAP

CGAP is a consortium of 28 public and private development agencies working together to expand access to financial services for the poor in developing countries. CGAP was created by these aid agencies and industry leaders to help create permanent financial services for the poor on a large scale (often referred to as "microfinance"). CGAP's unique membership structure and network of worldwide partners make it a potent convening platform to generate global consensus on standards and norms. As such, CGAP is a resource center for the entire microfinance industry, where it incubates and supports new ideas, innovative products, cutting-edge technology, novel mechanisms for deliving financial services, and concrete solutions to the challenges of expanding microfinance.

ABOUT INFODEV

infoDev is an international consortium of official bilateral and multilateral development agencies and other key partners, facilitated by an expert Secretariat housed at the World Bank. InfoDev's mission is to help developing countries and their partners in the international community use information and communication technologies (ICT) effectively and strategically as tools to combat poverty, promote sustainable economic growth, and empower individuals and communities to participate more fully and creatively in their societies and economies.

ABOUT IFC

The International Finance Corporation (IFC) promotes sustainable private sector investment in developing countries as a way to reduce poverty and improve people's lives. Established in 1956, IFC is the largest multilateral source of loan and equity financing for private sector projects in the developing world. It promotes sustainable private sector development primarily by financing private sector projects and providing advice and technical assistance to businesses and governments in the developing world.

IFC is a member of the World Bank Group and is headquartered in Washington, DC. It shares the primary objective of all World Bank Group institutions: to improve the quality of the lives of people in its developing member countries.

ABOUT THE AUTHORS

David Keogh

David's focus is on connectivity, access to information, and new technology-driven enterprise opportunities for micro-entrepreneurs. Before joining the Grameen Technology Center, he worked in the field of microfinance as the associate director of business development and policy at FINCA International. David has worked as a project manager, engineering consultant, and wireless communications developer. David first came to the United States on a fellowship while he completed his MBA and worked for Collins Commercial Aviation on electronic hardware design and software development. David graduated with an honors degree in digital systems and computer engineering from the Royal Melbourne Institute of Technology in Melbourne, Australia.

Tim Wood

Tim specializes in applying information technology to address the problems of poverty and health in developing countries. After 12 years at Microsoft working on software development, Tim spent two years working with the Bill & Melinda Gates Foundation where he defined the Information Technology Strategy for their Global Health Program and reviewed grant proposals. He joined the Grameen Technology Center in 2002 to focus on replicating the Grameen Village Phone program. Tim brings a broad range of technical and business expertise, and a valued perspective on technology initiatives for developing countries. He received a B.A. in Political Science from Stanford University.

CONTENTS

FOREWORD

When we first developed the program, many professionals were skeptical about the capacity of illiterate people to understand and use state-of-the-art telecommunication technology. Today Grameen Bank – which has 150,000 village phone ladies and will have 200,000 by the end of the year -- proved them wrong. The replication in Uganda – still quite small but growing rapidly -- clearly shows that information and communications technology is needed by all, regardless of income status. Village Phone fosters meaningful, lasting change in people's lives. It brings economic benefit to the local entrepreneurs who run the service like a public pay phone system, gives their communities greater access to government services and markets for their products, and connects them with friends and relatives living in other areas.

In the continuing march towards globalization, the world's poor must not be left behind. Information and communications technology can dramatically change their fate if we can ensure access.

The success of Village Phone replication in Uganda clearly demonstrate that the Village Phone concept can be replicated and customized in other countries where there are willing partners and strong support. In this effort, the microfinance institution has been the critical link. Its deep roots opened these rural communities to telecommunications.

In the developed world, many take telephone access for granted. But for those in many developing countries, particularly the rural poor, these communication services are extremely limited or non-existent. The experiences in Bangladesh and Uganda demonstrate how a relatively inexpensive technology can solve many of the problems the poor have faced for decades. These successes have no international boundaries and this replication manual is an excellent guide for introducing the program in new countries. As we celebrate the UN's International Year of Microcredit, I hope the global community will recognize its value and actively use information and communications technology in efforts to end global poverty.

Professor Muhammad Yunus
Founder and Managing Director, Grameen Bank

PREFACE

The publication of this book is very timely, for two principal reasons. First, the proven success of the Village Phone, as a multistakeholder project, convincingly illustrates the value of partnership amongst multiple stakeholders having diverse goals. Promoting ICT for development by building partnerships among governments, civil society, the private sector, and international and local organizations has been a primary goal of the Task Force since its inception in 2001. The greatest potential for enhancing the development impact of ICT lies in such partnerships, and the Task Force has been actively forging these relationships, in particular through its regional networks and thematic working groups.

Secondly, this "Replication Manual" is an invaluable how-to source for setting up a Village Phone project. It contains a realistic, practical, and detailed set of instructions, templates, and lessons learned, and it is generic enough to be applied in any context where a Village Phone initiative can help empower people and promote development. The insights are based on extensive research and learned practice, and while local adaptations will always be necessary, this manual provides a head start that will save time and money. It is my hope that this manual will be used and adapted in the many places around the world still untouched by modern communication technology and will thus contribute to the achievement of development goals.

As the authors emphasize, a strong partnership between telecommunications providers, microcredit institutions, the Village Phone company and operators is indispensable for the success of Village Phone. By crafting a "win-win" situation for all participants, productive and sustainable operation of the partnership is ensured. Charity or government fiat is not required to bring about social good. Instead, by creating a model in which the phone company wins, the micro-credit organizations win, the village phone operator wins, and the villagers themselves win, the model becomes self-sustained. It can be replicated on a national scale, as it has been in Bangladesh and Uganda. Village Phone proves that profitability and development are complementary, not antagonistic.

The Village Phone project also highlights the crucial nexus between business, technology, and development, another theme the Task Force has been promoting. We know that entrepreneurship is indispensable for lifting people out of poverty. It empowers them and gives them control over their lives and livelihood. By adding technology - in the form of the humble cellular phone - to the mix, Village Phone succeeded in creating entrepreneurs, connecting a village to the world, and earning a profit while doing so.

I strongly believe that Village Phone is an example to be replicated, but the lessons learned go much further than cellular phones and partnership structures. Using a model similar to Village Phone, a whole host of development interventions with diverse services in rural areas are possible. If partnerships and "win-win" solutions have proven to be so successful in the villages of Uganda and Bangladesh, what could not be potentially achieved if we build on this experience and use our creative thinking in the broader development realm? We are only limited by our imagination. The principal goal of the ICT Task Force is to promote, through dialogue, such creative thinking and advance the creation of an inclusive information society by bringing together governments, the private sector, civil society, international organizations and, most importantly, citizens around shared objectives.

Village Phone is ahead of its time and is leading the way by example. We should learn from this experience, emulate it and find ways to bring the benefits of partnership, cooperation, and communication to the billions so far untouched by the information revolution.

Sarbuland Khan
Director, Division for ECOSOC Support and Coordination, and Executive
Coordinator of the Secretariat of the United Nations ICT Task Force

INTRODUCTION

Few things are as central to life today, as the ability to make a phone call.

It is something most of us take completely for granted—but something that millions of poor people in the villages of the developing world can rarely do.

With no access to fixed-line telecommunications infrastructure, they cannot call a doctor when a child is sick, determine fair market prices for their crops, or easily contact family members in their capital city. The resulting isolation from today's information-driven economy is a major factor contributing to their poverty and marginalization.

The advent of affordable mobile communications has begun to change all this. In several low-income countries there are now more cell phones in use than installed lines. In the case of Grameen Village Phone, we see how the forces of innovation and the marketplace can widen the impact on this trend even further, improving living standards for large numbers of people by integrating entrepreneurship, microfinance, and mobile communications.

It is an important proven model ready for broader replication. This manual is designed to be a tool for doing so, although we must remember that any attempt to reapply this model in a new country will involve its own challenges, requiring careful preparation and planning. Our organizations are ready to assist with that.

Bangladesh now has more than 125,000 new Village Phone Operators in place—mostly poor village women. They have seen their incomes and status in the community increase dramatically by selling pooled cell phone time to their peers, using equipment that costs no more than US$250 at start-up. Pioneered by one of the world's best known microfinance organizations, Grameen Bank, it is a highly successful program, but one that until MTN villagePhone in Uganda had never been replicated in another country. Doing so required extensive and complex efforts.

Our three organizations were pleased to support Grameen Foundation USA's work to take this unique model to Uganda, which had only 1.72 phones (both fixed-line and installed) for every 100 people when this project began. Within 12 months of operation, Village Phone operators were selling an average of six times more airtime than was consumed by a typical subscriber of the local cellular provider, MTN Uganda. As in Bangladesh, a business model that combined microfinance and mobile communications proved highly effective in generating consumer demand.

Grameen Village Phone is a remarkable case study in development. The process of identifying the critical success factors necessary to take the original Bangladesh example and replicate it under Uganda's vastly different situation has resulted in an important contribution. Our hope with this manual now is to provide the lessons learned, technical information, and other materials necessary to those others who may want to carry this work further. .

Laurence Carter
Director, Small and Medium Enterprise Department, World Bank Group

Elizabeth Littlefield
Director and CEO, CGAP,

Mostafa Terrab
Program Manager, Information for Development (infoDev)

INTRODUCING THE VILLAGE PHONE REPLICATION MANUAL

This document is a guideline for replicating the Village Phone program in a new country. It draws on Grameen's experience in both Bangladesh and Uganda and establishes a template for creating sustainable initiatives that simultaneously bring telecommunications to the rural poor, create viable new businesses for micro-entrepreneurs, and expand the customer base of telecommunications companies.

No two implementations of the Village Phone program will be exactly alike. Each country will have unique variables, participants, and environments. However, it is expected that there will be common structures, applications, and processes – all of which are described in detail herein.

The information presented in this replication manual is shared in the spirit of international cooperation. Grameen Foundation USA will continue to act as a clearinghouse for Village Phone Replication information. As people share the lessons from future replication efforts, Grameen Foundation USA will publish updates to reflect additional learning.

VILLAGE PHONE

The Need for Village Phones

Most people in developed countries take for granted their ability to contact others by telephone. However, in developing countries, access to communication services can be extremely challenging, especially for the rural poor. Given the high cost of deploying telecommunications infrastructure, governments and industry have little financial incentive to extend communications networks to rural areas in developing countries. As a result, millions live without the ability to contact people beyond their local village.

In rural areas there are often no affordable and accessible telecommunications services. Telecommunications providers are reticent to place public access telephone booths in these locations as the initial investment and ongoing maintenance costs do not make for a viable business proposition. Governments, through their regulators, often place "Universal Access" requirements on telecommunications providers. These requirements result in an infrastructure investment that can make access available to some degree. These services typically operate at a loss and the telecommunications provider maintains them as a duty to their licensing obligation.

Why is it such a challenge to provide telecommunications to rural areas? High initial infrastructure investment, relative low call volumes, high maintenance costs due to harsh environments, cash box collection needs, cash security costs (for coin operated phones), card availability (for prepaid airtime systems), technical illiteracy, remote locations, and high transportation costs are just some of the impediments to providing rural telecommunications access.

Village Phone addresses these issues. It provides a profitable new market niche for telecommunications companies, new and profitable micro-enterprises for rural poor Village Phone Operators, and affordable and accessible access for communities.

What is Village Phone?

Village Phone is a methodology that creates a profitable partnership and a channel to market to bring telecommunications services to the rural areas of a developing nation. It offers a framework to extend telecommunication service to the rural poor in countries where an investment has already been made in mobile phone infrastructure. Village Phone is based on a business model that is sustainable for all of the participants and enables the poorest of the poor to have access to valuable communication services. Additionally, through this telecommunications service, rural individuals can gain access to information that increases their productivity, earns better prices for the goods they produce, and saves on the direct and opportunity costs of traveling away from home.

> *Village Phone is a methodology that creates a profitable partnership and a channel to market to bring telecommunications services to the rural areas of a developing nation.*

By leapfrogging fixed infrastructure and leveraging existing wireless infrastructure, Village Phones offer a viable strategy for increasing teledensity in developing countries and helping the poor lift themselves out of poverty.

How Village Phone Works

In many rural villages there are no telecommunications services, no public phone booths, no private subscriber fixed lines, and no individual who owns a mobile handset. People have no option but to physically travel to communicate. Studies have shown that there can be a cost to *not* making a phone call – up to eight times more expensive than the cost of the actual phone call. The rural poor cannot make telephone calls simply because there is no access, not because they cannot afford to or don't wish to.

The cost of developing and maintaining an infrastructure to place telephones in these rural areas often prohibits telecommunications operators from entering this market. Another barrier is the lack of a mechanism that allows them to interact with their customers, selling airtime and making financial transactions. What is missing is essentially a 'channel' that would allow Telecom Operators to connect with their potential market.

> *The rural poor cannot make telephone calls simply because there is no access - not because they cannot afford to or don't wish to!*

By their very nature, microfinance institutions have deep roots into rural communities. They are trusted institutions with detailed knowledge of the local communities and an existing infrastructure for regularly visiting these communities to transact financial services with their rural clients. These deep links into the community are essential for introducing new services and the potential contribution of microfinance institutions to new business initiatives targeting rural communities is often undervalued. Here is a 'channel to market' to bring telecommunications services to the rural poor.

The microfinance sector is historically missing from telecommunication operators' normal distribution chain. By utilizing microfinance institutions as a channel to market, the telecommunications industries in Bangladesh and Uganda were able to tap a market that was previously inaccessible because of the prohibitively high cost of developing and maintaining a channel to this enormous market.

As a member of a microfinance institution (MFI), a potential Village Phone Operator uses a loan to purchase everything needed to start their business. The Village Phone starter kit costs approximately US$200-US$250 and includes a mobile phone, prepaid airtime card, external Yagi antenna, charging solution, signage, marketing collateral, and other materials necessary to get started. The Starter Kit is created by the "Village Phone Company", which establishes relationships with microfinance institutions to bring this product to their customers. The Village Phone Company negotiates wholesale airtime rates from the Telecommunications Provider who provides access to existing telecommunications infrastructure for the Village Phone Operators. Individual villagers in rural areas can then visit their local Village Phone Operator and make an affordable phone call.

With proceeds from the business, the Village Phone Operator contributes to their loan repayment and also purchases additional prepaid airtime cards. The microfinance institution earns money from the loan and also a percentage of the revenue from airtime sales. The Telecommunications Provider earns money through volume sales of airtime, and the Village Phone Company earns enough money to continue to promote and expand the program. There are no subsidies in this model. It works because it is designed so that all parties in the partnership "win".

Village Phone Roles and Responsibilities

Microfinance Institution

- Credit finance to Village Phone Operator
- Conduit for prepaid airtime to Village Phone Operators
- Conduit for equipment to Village Phone Operators
- Village Phone Operator training
- Strategic Planning with partners
- Customer support when phone is inoperable
- Monitor appropriate use of phones and prepaid cards

Telecommunications Provider

- Communications Infrastructure
- Provide and validate communications coverage to needed rural areas
- Prepaid airtime supply to MFI
- Usage reporting
- Government licensing and regulation compliance and liaison
- Government financial and taxation liaison
- On-air customer support
- Strategic Planning with partners
- Source equipment from suppliers

Village Phone Company

- General problem solving
- Financial Management
- Monitor overall program progress
- Drive and plan network expansion
- Strategic planning
- Village Phone Operator Monitoring
- Partner reporting
- Media coordination
- Training of MFI Staff
- Evaluation and Analysis
- Knowledge consolidation and dissemination
- Replication model development
- Partner development - creating linkages and business relationships for program expansion

Village Phone Operator

- Marketing
- Channel to Market
- User Billing and collection
- Airtime purchases
- Providing communications service to the community
- A communications knowledge resource to the community
- Equipment maintenance

SUCCESS IN BANGLADESH

One of the greatest success stories in international development has been Grameen's Village Phone program in Bangladesh. In rural villages where no telecommunications service has previously existed, mobile phones are provided to very poor women who use the phone to operate as a business. These micro-entrepreneurs purchase the phone with a loan from Grameen Bank and then sell the use of it on a per call basis. The benefits to both the operator and the community have been tremendous. The typical "village phone lady" has an average income three times the national average.

The most obvious benefit of the Village Phone program is the economic impact that this communications tool brings to the entire village. There is clear evidence of this impact in Bangladesh, including higher prices paid to Village Phone users for their goods and better exchange rates when repatriating funds. For the cost of a phone call, a family is able to save the expense of sending a productive member to deliver or retrieve information by traveling great distances in person. Some creative and entrepreneurial users of the technology identify new business opportunities, including the resale of information to others in their communities. The technology also serves to link regional entrepreneurs with each other and their clients, bringing more business to small enterprises. Phones have even been used in emergency situations, such as accessing medical assistance during natural disasters.

> *"Farmers from the villages use the phones to call the city markets to find out prices for their produce. Previously they were a little bit short-changed by their middlemen. The middlemen would say a lower price than what the actual market price was. So now they can call the market themselves to find out what the actual price of eggs or whatever their produce is. An independent study found that half the people who use the phones regularly, traders in rice or bananas for example, make more money from their business and they save 10 hours in travel time."* [1]

> *"If the Grameen Telecom experience is a reliable guide, then providing phone service yields powerful social and economic benefits in rural communities....Empowering poor communities by providing a wide range of digitally enabled self-help tools — via the private sector — could become a crucial part of an effective rural development strategy ... Business is a proven method of solving their [poor individuals] problems in a sustainable way."* [2]

In a Canadian International Development Agency (CIDA) commissioned study[3], it was concluded that the Grameen Village Phone program yields "significant positive social and economic impacts, including relatively large consumer surplus and immeasurable quality of life benefits". The study concluded that the consumer surplus for a single phone call ranges from 2.64% to 9.8% of mean monthly household income. The cost of a trip to the city ranges from two to eight times the

---

[1] NPR Marketplace September 25, 2002
[2] Iqbal Quadir, Co-Founder of GrameenPhone and Lecturer in Public Policy at Harvard University
[3] Grameen Telecom's Village Phone Programme in Rural Bangladesh: a Multi Media Case Study. Canadian International Development Agency, March 2000

cost of a single phone call, meaning that the real savings for poor rural people is between \$2.70 and \$10.00 for individual calls. The income that Village Phone Operators derive from the Village Phone is about 24% of the household income on average – in some cases it was as high as 40% of the household income.

Because the phone operators are typically female and the phones are in their places of business, women who might otherwise have very limited access to a phone feel comfortable using Village Phones. Furthermore, as these phones become important for the whole village, the status of women in the communities where they work is enhanced.

> "Phones have helped elevate the status of the female phone operators in the village. Surveys have found that the Village Phone Operators become socially empowered as they earn an income, gaining participation in family decisions in which, in rural Bangladeshi society, women usually have no say." [4]

> "... [Grameen Village Phone] has had considerable development benefits. It has reduced the cost of communications relative to other services such as transportation....the program has enabled the village pay phone entrepreneurs, poor by most standards but among the better-off in their villages, to turn a profit." [5]

Having established the infrastructure and institutional framework for such a venture, the poor become the drivers of their own destiny and the experts in the utilization of this technology to their own best advantages – telecommunications is a powerful catalyst and facilitator of such grassroots, self-directed development :

> "Isolation and lack of information [communications] are very serious obstacles to poverty eradication" – Masud Isa, Managing Director of Grameen Telecom

> "People lack many things: jobs, shelter, food, health care, and drinkable water. Today, being cut off from basic telecommunications services is a hardship almost as acute as these other deprivations, and may indeed reduce the chances of finding remedies to them."
> – Kofi Anan, United Nations Secretary General [6]

Grameen's Village Phone program in Bangladesh has been incredibly successful, with over 110,000 Village Phone Operators [7] in place who have established a clear path out of the cycle of poverty. However, despite the tremendous success in Bangladesh, a Village Phone initiative has never been successfully replicated in another country – until now.

---

[4] World Resources Institute, 2002
[5] The World Bank Group - Public Policy for the Private Sector. Note No. 205, March 2000. Bringing Cellular Phone Service to Rural Areas.
[6] The U.S. National Commission on Libraries and Information Science speech at Telecom 99 in Geneva, Switzerland, UN Secretary General Kofi Anan
[7] as of February 2005

REPLICATION IN UGANDA

Although cellular phone network coverage extends into a majority of rural Uganda, very few people in rural areas can afford to purchase a mobile phone. The teledensity in Uganda is approximately 1.72 (1.72 telephones for every 100 people)[8]. These telephones are concentrated in urban areas, making rural access to telecommunications difficult and costly; this despite the fact that only 14% of the Uganda's population lives in urban centers. Cut off from easy access to information, poor rural Ugandans are placed at an economic and social disadvantage. For example, middlemen who come to purchase their goods often pay rates significantly below market rates. With access to telecommunication services, rural farmers can be aware of and receive fair market value for their goods, entrepreneurs in neighboring villages can consolidate their buying power for raw materials and services, and friends and family can be quickly contacted.

In February 2002, the Grameen Technology Center, an initiative of Grameen Foundation USA, launched an initiative to replicate the success of the Village Phone program outside of Bangladesh. Uganda, with its flourishing micro-finance organizations and strong mobile telecommunications infrastructure, was identified as the first country for replication. This innovative initiative had four simultaneous goals:

1. to provide the rural communities of Uganda with valuable communications services to enable them to break the cycle of poverty
2. to validate, measure, and document the Village Phone model in a single country outside of Bangladesh
3. to establish a generalized replication model for the Village Phone program
4. to disseminate this learning to the commercial telecommunications sector and the worldwide development communities so as to catalyze and establish a global Village Phone movement.

The Grameen Technology Center approached MTN Uganda, Uganda's leading mobile telecommunications provider, in March of 2002 to propose working together to extend telecommunication services to rural Uganda. The proposed business model for Uganda recommended working in partnership with the Ugandan microfinance sector and detailed a viable revenue model for a Ugandan Village Phone program. Detailed discussions between Grameen, MTN Uganda, and MTN publiCom (MTN's partnership that focuses on public access telecommunications) took place. Simultaneously, partnerships with multiple microfinance institutions were explored. In March 2003, the MTN Uganda Board of Directors ratified the Business Model and a 'Heads of Agreement' outlining the terms of the partnership and the first ten phones were deployed in the Masindi district. Additional microfinance partners were engaged, and by September 2003, 100 phones had been deployed. A pilot phase to test the viability of the business model was conducted and successfully completed in October 2003.

---

[8] World Telecommunication Development Report, ITU, 2002

In November 2003, MTN villagePhone was formally created and launched as an independent company, "a sustainable initiative that aims to alleviate poverty and empower rural Ugandans through the provision of communications services."[9] Twelve months into formal operations, Village Phone operators in Uganda were selling an average of six times more airtime than is consumed by a typical MTN Uganda subscriber.

Keys for success

There are four vital elements to ensure the long-term success of a Village Phone program:

1. The program should be structured so that all parties benefit. This can be in quantifiable economic terms and in also in other more intangible ways. For example, while the Telecommunications Operator benefits financially (revenue from a previously unreached market niche), their constituents also see them as being socially responsible. Telecommunications companies often have a "Corporate Social Responsibility Mandate" which Village Phone can help fulfill. The additional public relations the program generates also helps their image as an industry leader and increases market exposure. The Village Phone Operator owns a profitable business and also builds status in their community as a communications and information nexus. If they are female, their pivotal community role often serves to increase the overall status of women in the community.
2. The microfinance sector should be used as a 'channel to market'. These institutions have a trusted relationship with the rural communities and have a foundation for conducting financial transactions which occur on a regular basis. The social structures encouraged by microfinance institutions through groups, centers, and solidarity guarantees create a ready-made market for end-user consumers.
3. The telecommunications provider should provide wholesale airtime rates to Village Phone Operators to allow them to provide affordable services while simultaneously earning enough margin to repay their loan.
4. In-country staff should manage the business.

All Parties Win

A number of different parties need to collaborate in order to establish a successful Village Phone program. The Village Phone program succeeds by structuring mutually beneficial relationships that allow each partner to profit from the program.

---

[9] Yvonne Muthien, group executive of corporate affairs at MTN Uganda, http://www.itweb.co.za/sections/telecoms/2003/0311201205.asp?A=AFN&S=All%20Africa%20New s&O=E&CiRestriction

Partner	Essential Service Provided	How they "win"
Telecommunications Company	Communications infrastructure coverage to needed rural areas	New revenue generated from airtime sales from a previously inaccessible market
Microfinance Institution	Provide loans to Village Phone operators so they can purchase equipment to start a Village Phone business	Income from loans and airtime sales and a new product to market to clients
Village Phone Operator	Affordable telecommunications to members of their community	Profitable business which earns a steady income
Community members	Customer base for Village Phone Operators	Access to affordable telecommunications
Village Phone company	Crafts and manages relationships, facilitates support, manages overall program	Long-term success of program, sustainable (profitable) operation

It is important to note that each of the "wins" is quantifiable in monetary terms. In both Bangladesh and Uganda, the telecommunications partner is able to provide wholesale airtime rates because of the high volume of calls generated by the Village Phones. Village Phones are used up to eight times more than the phones of average subscriber in both countries. Rural markets are usually untapped, and the Village Phone program creates a new revenue stream for the telecommunications companies.

Microfinance institutions need to offer loan products that will enable entrepreneurs to succeed while also minimizing loan defaults. In this way, new capital comes back into the microfinance institution to provide to new borrowers. In the seven year history of the Village Phone program in Bangladesh, over 98% of Village Phone Operators repaid their loan in full – a phenomenal success rate. Similar numbers have been seen in the first twelve months of operations in Uganda. The program is also structured to provide the microfinance institution with a percentage of airtime sales. This mechanism provides a great incentive to establish and support as many strong, successful Village Phone businesses as possible.

At the local level, the entrepreneurs who decide to become Village Phone Operators must see a return on their investment for the business to be sustainable. A typical Village Phone Operator in Bangladesh has an income three times the national average. Their customers must see value as well, or else they will not spend their hard-earned money on a phone call. While market information and arranging business services clearly have a direct impact, for rural villagers the reduced opportunity cost alone is often of sufficient value, as they no longer have to travel many hours simply to make a call.

This "win-win-win-win-win" partnership ensures the long-term success of the Village Phone program.

Partner with the Microfinance sector as a channel to market

To reach markets previously thought unreachable, an innovative approach is needed. It is not feasible to develop from scratch a distribution channel to reach the rural market niche, and alternatives must be found: channels which already exist. Microfinance institutions have this distribution channel in place, albeit for financial services (and in some instances training and other services). This is a perfect match for Village Phone as weekly financial transactions and consumer contact are already occurring weekly within the structures of socially cohesive networks, self bonding, and self guaranteeing. Microfinance "hub and spoke structures" efficiently reach even the deepest rural areas, making this partnership a natural fit for Village Phone.

The microfinance institutions benefit from this collaboration as well. Village Phones are a new product that can be brought to the microfinance clients, generating loan income for the microfinance institution and positioning the microfinance institution as an innovative leader in the community. In addition, a revenue sharing plan for Village Phones can result in additional income. Microfinance institutions see Village Phone as being entirely consistent with their social mission by bringing the benefits of information and communications technology to their membership.

Wholesale airtime rates from the Telecommunications Company

In order to operate a viable business, the Village Phone Operators must be able to offer services at a competitive rate while simultaneously earning a margin to contribute to the repayment of their loan from the microfinance institution. The only way for these two conditions to be met is if the telecommunications company provides wholesale airtime rates to the Village Phone Operators.

Volume makes the discount economically viable for the telecommunications company. The average Village Phone in Bangladesh is used six times more per day than other phones. The average revenue per user (ARPU) of Village Phone subscribers in Bangladesh is double than that of the average business user.[10] In Uganda, the average revenue per user (ARPU) of Village Phone subscribers is seven times that of the average prepaid subscriber.

In-country staff are essential

When starting a new venture, there is no substitute for having individuals working in-country to actively drive activities forward. During the replication effort in Uganda, we found the pace of decision making increased significantly when Grameen Technology Center staff were in Uganda. To mitigate the impact of distance, Grameen hired three short-term consultants to work in Uganda for six months to help get the program off the ground. Their contribution was essential for laying the

---

[10] http://www.grameenphone.com/village.htm (July 2004)

operational groundwork for the Village Phone Company, establishing relationships with microfinance institutions, training and deploying the first wave of phone businesses in the rural communities with Village Phone Operators.

STEPS FOR REPLICATION OF VILLAGE PHONE

No two implementations of Village Phone will be identical. Each country will have unique features that call for variants in the division of roles, responsibilities and operations to be consistent with the local environment. The model developed for Uganda is not a 'cookie cutter' template; however, this particular incarnation of Village Phone and the environment in which it exists will most probably be closer to any future replication than the original Bangladeshi program. For example, it is unlikely there will be a single microfinance institution with sufficient membership to warrant an exclusive relationship, and unlike the GrameenPhone/Grameen Telecom Village Phone program, many of the worlds telecommunications operators are using pre-paid platforms.

Nevertheless, a common set of basic steps present themselves in the creation of a Village Phone program. Although these steps are presented here as separate efforts, there is a high degree of parallel development of concepts, agreements and coordination between the steps.

Step 1:	Identify a Target Country
Step 2:	Business Analysis and Financial Model Development
Step 3:	Identify Stakeholders and Relationships
Step 4:	Structuring the Company
Step 5:	Financing Village Phone
Step 6:	Establish Operational Foundation
Step 7:	Equipment Selection and Sourcing
Step 8:	Developing a Training Curriculum
Step 9:	Pilot Program
Step 10:	Hire Staff
Step 11:	Formal Launch
Step 12:	Marketing
Step 13:	Ongoing Operations
Step 14:	Sharing Best Practices

STEPS FOR REPLICATION – 1: IDENTIFY A TARGET COUNTRY

The first step is to determine an appropriate country for introducing the Village Phone program. There are a number of complimentary components that feed into this selection. These can be broken down into three broad categories: Fundamentals, Drivers and Other Factors:

Fundamentals

Fundamentals are necessary elements which MUST be present in the target country. They are:

1. Enabling regulatory environment
2. Willing and enthusiastic partners
3. Market potential.

1) Enabling Regulatory Environment

This is a rather subjective assessment of the political suitability for a Village Phone initiative, given that it must exist as a business entity and should be free to operate in such a manner that will facilitate its own success. Elements to consider are: ease of foreign investment and repatriation of investments, taxation, extent of privatization, laissez-faire policy, political influence on private enterprise, corruption, currency stability, and political stability. It is especially beneficial if the government has created policies that actively encourage telecommunications providers to invest in rural infrastructure development and require a universal service program.

2) Willing and Enthusiastic Partners

Multiple partners are required to create a successful Village Phone initiative, and each of these partners must be willing to invest time and energy into the program for it to be successful. If the partners are only marginally interested, or at a stage in their institutional development that does not allow them to fully embrace Village Phone, then the program will fail. Institutional focus from the top, sufficient management bandwidth, and a culture that is able to innovate are all essential.

It is very difficult to catalyze new partnerships when operating from abroad. Even when operating locally and independently, it can be challenging to generate the necessary momentum to launch a new product initiative. Efforts must be made to keep the pivotal partners engaged and to make sure they continually have a 'stake in the game'.

The strong partnerships and shared common vision were critical for the success of Village Phone in Bangladesh and Uganda. Bangladesh could be considered unique in that all three critical partners share common Grameen 'DNA'. It could be argued that the only reason that Village Phone worked in Bangladesh was because of an overarching governing mission and cohesiveness of these three organizations.

Village Phone in Uganda proved that this was not true and that Village Phone can thrive with multiple "unrelated" partners.

The partnership with the Telecommunications Operator is definitely the most critical. We found the best way to maintain a strong relationship with the telecommunications operator was to not play across the sector and instead, forge a partnership with a single provider. The Telecommunications Operator must have a significant stake in the success of the program to ensure their long-term engagement.

On the other hand, to create a market of sufficient size for Village Phone to reach scale, both in terms of sustainability and profitability, in Uganda it was necessary to work across the microfinance sector with multiple partners. While managing multiple partnerships can be time consuming, our experience in Uganda has shown that it is viable.

3) Market Potential

Village Phone must be considered holistically. At each level of operations, sustainability and profitability must be assured. If one component of the model falls short, the system does not support itself. For example, while an individual Village Phone Operator may be successful, the infrastructure that must support a formal network of Village Phone operators may not be present. The key factor here is simply numbers and scale – specifically the number of Village Phones in use and the utilization of each phone. If the model cannot be structured to allow sufficient revenue to flow to cover operational costs for the Village Phone Company and provide a significant return on investment for the partners, then one must carefully consider if this is the right environment for Village Phone replication.

Drivers

Drivers are elements that determine the potential and success of Village Phone. Specifically:

1. Telecommunications coverage in the target rural areas
2. Microfinance outreach in the target rural areas
3. Correlation between these two primary drivers
4. Population density
5. Rural telecommunications demand
6. Existing Teledensity
7. Poverty demographics
8. Viable options to Village Phone (Competition)
9. Cost of phone calls

Existing telecommunications coverage in the target rural areas

The Village Phone model relies on using existing telecommunications infrastructure to provide service. Given the high cost of building out this infrastructure (each GSM mobile phone communications base station costs up to $250,000), it would not be economically viable for a telecommunications company to build base stations only to serve a sparsely populated rural area.

For GSM-based networks, we are able to extend the usable range for a handset by using an external antenna. It is theoretically possible to extend the functional range of a base station up to 35km, reaching well into rural areas. Typically a handset's utility (e.g., call quality, drop-outs) reduces as it is moved beyond 15 kilometers from a base station – shorter if the terrain is mountainous as GSM relies on "line of sight". Village Phones deployed with an external antenna between 15 and 35km from a base station can operate in an almost monopoly environment. As phones approach the limit of 35 kilometers, call quality will degrade and in some instances phones will not be usable. There are also other factors that practically limit the distance from the base station: foliage, terrain, rain (or other atmospheric occlusions), curvature of the earth, height of the transmitting and receiving antennas, handset power output, alignment of receiving antenna, electrical properties at each antenna cable connection point, and system frequency. Even though the GSM system in Uganda is 900/1800 MHz, we have chosen single band Yagi antennas tuned to 900MHZ as this gives slightly better range and signal strength. There are of course a myriad of parameters which will impact the performance of a Village Phone.

In both Bangladesh and Uganda, the predominant technology is 900/1800 MHz GSM. However, there is no technical constraint to using other technologies for a Village Phone program. CDMA technology is currently being used in Uganda alongside GSM for Village Phone.

In 2002, MTN Uganda's existing infrastructure reached approximately 50% of the country's population and service extended into many rural areas. The company was installing new base stations at a rate of approximately one per week, steadily increasing the reach of the MTN communications network. Despite MTN's broad coverage, rural access to telecommunications service in Uganda was fairly limited. The teledensity for Uganda was 1.72 (1.72 telephones - fixed and wireless - for every 100 people) and the waiting list for access to a fixed line telephone was 3.6 years.[11]

Strength, Outreach and Operating Environment of the Microfinance Sector

---

[11] World Telecommunications Development Report – ITU 2002

It is important to understand how strong the microfinance institutions are in a country as these organizations will serve as the primary channel to market for Village Phones. Specifically:

- How many microfinance organizations are operating in the country?
- Is there a coordinating association / forum that works across the sector?
- How many clients does each of these organizations have?
- Are the clients in rural areas (vs. urban or peri-urban)?
- What services do these clients use? Are they predominantly borrowers, savers, or both?
- What are the methodologies typically used (Solidarity Groups, Village Banking, Grameen, Individual, etc.)?
- How mature is the sector as a whole?
- Is the sector committed to "Microfinance Best Practices"?
- Are there distortions in the sector caused by some microfinance institutions offering subsidized services?
- Are donors supporting the microfinance institution sector? Is funding available? How 'liquid' is the sector?
- What is the growth potential for the market? What percentage of the market is currently served?
- What are the average effective interest rates and range of rates for the microfinance institution sector?
- What are the typical loan durations offered by the microfinance institutions?
- How much overlap in coverage exists between microfinance institutions? Is there competition between microfinance institutions? What are the differentiators?
- Are microfinance institutions 'Credit Only', 'Financial Services', or Business Development Services (BDS)'?
- Are microfinance institutions offering 'Credit +', education, health?
- Are there any regulatory barriers for microfinance institution participation in Village Phone?

Answers to these questions are very challenging to find and often require a significant amount of research, contact networking and/or face-to-face meetings with the institutions in-country. Preliminary information can often be found on the Internet, for example:

- Microcredit Summit Campaign: http://www.microcreditsummit.org/
- Microfinance Information eXchange Market: http://www.mixmarket.org/
- PlanetFinance: http://planetfinance.org
- The Global Development Research Center: http://www.gdrc.org/icm/index.html
- MicroFinance Network: http://www.mfnetwork.org
- The Microfinance Gateway: http://www.microfinancegateway.org/
- United Nations Capital Development Fund: http://www.uncdf.org/english/microfinance/index.html

Other good sources of information are non-government organizations that work in the country (e.g. USAID, CIDA, European Union, UNDP, World Bank) or in-country industry associations (e.g. AMFIU - the Association Microfinance Institutions in Uganda).

The ideal market has a handful of medium to large microfinance institutions which have a high percentage of their clients in rural areas. It is advantageous if the microfinance institutions work in geographically distinct regions of the country to maximize coverage for the program. Prior to starting to work in Uganda, the market was estimated at 190,000 clients with 10 different organizations. Only after Grameen started working in Uganda was a better understanding attained of the microfinance sector – which programs were strongest and which operated in urban and rural areas.

Overlapping service areas

A market with both existing telecommunications coverage and a strong existing microfinance sector is not automatically appropriate for Village Phone. These two areas must overlap such that the existing telecommunication coverage exists in the rural areas where the microfinance institutions operate. A channel to market is useful only if it reaches the target market, and those people outside of existing telecommunications coverage are not a part of the initial target for Village Phone.

> *In two different locations in Uganda, the operators of payphones were charging customers double the posted rates (800/= vs. 350/=) as they controlled the cards that were inserted into these "public" phones. About 3km away from each of these locations, a Village Phone operator started a business. Quite quickly, people learned about the new Village Phone operators and began using their much more affordable services, saying that they "would rather walk the distance than be cheated by these people."*

Population density

On average, how many people live in a rural village? How far apart are villages from each other? How many people would a single Village Phone business in that village serve? These are all important questions when assessing how much revenue an average Village Phone Operator will be able to generate with their business. A Village Phone Operator who serves a community of 500 people is much more likely to be successful than the one who serves a community of 50. From the perspective of someone wishing to make a call, there is a tradeoff made between the distance the person is willing to travel, their opportunity cost, and the savings in making a call from a Village Phone as opposed to another entrepreneur.

The population density in Bangladesh is exceptionally high. As a result, it is rare for a Village Phone to be deployed in a rural village without experiencing immediate demand. In many instances, population densities are high enough to support more than one Village Phone operator per village (there are only 58,000 villages in Bangladesh, yet over 95,000 Village Phones have been deployed[12]).

In Bangladesh a 'village' averages around 2000 people or 400 households. This guideline was used in Uganda, where initially the objective was for each Village Phone Operator to also serve at least 2,000 people. With a much lower population density in Uganda, this suggested spacing Village Phone Operators at least 2km apart from one another. It is quite common for people to travel much further than 2km to use a Village Phone. Further research and analysis suggests that a community of approximately 100 households can support a Village Phone.

Rural Telecommunications Demand

A Village Phone program makes sense if easy access to affordable telecommunications services does not already exist in rural areas. A formal market survey can provide detailed information, but informal surveys of microfinance clients can also yield good insights into important variables. Important topics to cover in a survey are:

1. *Affordability:* How much are rural individuals currently paying to place a call? If telecommunications services are available, it is very likely that someone will be selling use of a personal mobile phone. However, while services may be available, access will not be reliable and the rates are usually extremely high. In Uganda we found individuals charging up to three times the going retail rate for a phone call with the price charged being dependent upon the urgency and need of the caller at that time. The poverty demographic and purchasing power of rural individuals obviously moderates this analysis - 'affordability' is not absolute, but relative.
2. If a one minute calls costs a poor rural villager up to 20% of their daily gross earnings for a day ($0.20 from a $1.00 per day income, for example), then a valid question would be "Why would they make that call?" The answer lies in the cost of the alternatives – A Canadian International Development Agency (CIDA) commissioned study[13], it was concluded that the consumer surplus for a single phone call ranges from 2.64% to 9.8% of mean monthly household income. The cost of a trip to the city ranges from two to eight times the cost of a single phone call, meaning significant savings for poor rural people.

---

[12] As of February 2005
[13] Grameen Telecom's Village Phone Programme in Rural Bangladesh: a Multi Media Case Study. Canadian International Development Agency, March 2000

3. *Accessibility:* How far do people need to travel in order to reach a location where they can place (and receive) a phone call? If a Village Phone can be placed in a location that saves many people from walking 5km, there will likely be strong demand for that business.

4. *Current teledensity:* How many individuals have telecommunication service in the rural areas? Often teledensity statistics are quoted without regard for urban and rural distinction. If (affordable) accessible phone service is common, there may be little need for public access phones.

5. *Nature of competitive services:* Are there any other organizations offering rural telecommunication services? What services are offered and at what price? How many different potential competitors exist? Are there any barriers to entry?

> Civil war has been a constant in northern Uganda for many years. The Lords Resistance Army (LRA) has been fighting a guerilla-style war with the Government of Uganda. The LRA often raid rural communities who have no advance warning and the consequences are deadly. Rose Atim is a Village Phone Operator in Lira district in northern Uganda. When the LRA rebels attacked her village of Barlonyo and massacred 200 people, she was able to flee because she received advance information from a friend who called on her villagePhone. She was able to escape into the fields and remain undiscovered until she heard on her phone that the coast was clear.

6. *Current Alternatives:* What do people do now to communicate? What is the opportunity cost of this alternative? It may be a public access phone booth, public transportation, messengers, letters, email or the many other traditional means of communicating.

In general, urban areas are not the best location for Village Phones. There tends to be a great deal of competition for telecommunication services in urban areas (often building on older fixed wire infrastructure), making it difficult for a Village Phone operator to generate enough income, and the opportunity costs for making a call are not as great as for those who live in rural areas.

Other Factors

Other factors which will influence the potential and success of Village Phone are:

1. *Telecom policy* which may dictate network interconnect rates, independence of the regulating body, residual competitive advantages of pre-privatization monopoly operator, and tariff structures (legality of charging for terminating as well as originating calls, mandated rural / urban pricing equity, tariff change and approval process)

2. *Design of Universal Access Fund* which may cause distortions in the competitive environment or create access to funds

3. *Taxation,* include VAT, excise taxes, and taxes for a Universal Access Fund

4. *Collective Social and Cultural Factors* which may include social cohesion, the culture of payment, trust between organizations, pre- and post-paid models

(multiple levels), prior collective experience with microfinance (best practice, government intervention, loan forgiveness, etc.), entrepreneurial spirit, literacy and numeracy

5. *Expatriate population.* International calls are typically higher margin and more expensive than domestic calls and hence assist in sustainability at all levels.

This is not an exhaustive list, but is intended to provide a starting point for analysis and suitability for a potential Village Phone initiative.

With a mission to empower the world's poorest to lift themselves out of poverty, Grameen Foundation USA has targeted countries that are extremely poor. The United Nations Human Development Reports (http://hdr.undp.org/reports/global/2003/indicator/index.html) are an excellent source of information.

STEPS FOR REPLICATION – 2: BUSINESS PLANNING, ANALYSIS AND FINANCIAL MODEL DEVELOPMENT

Before making any investment in establishing partnerships, it is important to validate that a Village Phone program can create a 'win' scenario for all constituents over the course of multiple years. This 'win' scenario is often discussed in terms of financial sustainability or profitability, but is not limited only to this measure of sustainability. To complete an early financial analysis, it is important to determine some of the most important variables:

- *Cost of mobile phone equipment.* The technical requirements for the wireless phone need to be established early to determine the price of the equipment the Village Phone Operator will be purchasing. For example, the mobile phone will likely require a connector for an external antenna. In some markets, the Telecommunications Operator may wish to validate the choice of phone handset or mandate a Payphone Management System (PMS).

- *Financing Costs.* A survey of the microfinance sector will determine what average financing costs will be for the Village Phone Operators.

- *Average number of minutes per day sold.* The population density of the country and extent of rural demand will be indicators to help estimate the average number of minutes per day a Village Phone Operator can sell. In Bangladesh, the average Village Phone Operator sells 57 minutes of incoming *and* outgoing calls. In Uganda, 20 min/day was used for early financial models as only outgoing calls are charged in the country.

- *Estimated number of Village Phone businesses to be created.* Based on the number of microfinance clients and the population of the country. This is important to determine projected usage rates.

- *Village Phone business creation rate (number of businesses established per month).* This will be a function of the number of microfinance partners, the telecommunications coverage, and the number of staff available to deploy Village Phone starter kits.

- *Operational expenses for Village Phone Company.* The number of staff and vehicles required will likely be the largest expenses for the Village Phone Company. A "Sample Business Model" is available in Appendix I which details the expenses.
- *Wholesale and retail tariffs and margins for partners.* These numbers are the basis for revenue and sustainability projections.

From these numbers, spreadsheets should be created that model the entire business for all of the parties involved in the Village Phone program, including income, expenses, and net revenue. Be sure to take into account in-country taxation, any Value Added Taxation (VAT), excise tax and other externally-imposed outgoing cash flows from the business. It is also very important to look at the timing and point of payment for these items. Cash flow management becomes critical for a business such as this, and while a profitable business may have been modeled, it will struggle month-to-month if there is not sufficient cash flow to pay creditors. Negotiate favorable terms with creditors and debtors and build in buffers and allowances to the model to accommodate any country-specific banking system deficiencies, cultural tendencies for delaying payment, or other typical business perturbations.

It is also important to establish the financial and philosophical goals for the program. In Uganda, our financial goal was for the Village Phone Company to begin generating an operating profit in the third year of operations after establishing approximately two thousand Village Phone businesses.

There are multiple levels at which this business operates and all must be viable in their own right. There are no subsidies in this business model and each aspect of the overall system operates profitably and sustainably. Consider the model at the various levels:

Project Partner	Business Model
Telecommunications Company	Airtime sales yield profits on prior infrastructure investments The Telecommunications Company wishes to reach a greater customer base in poor rural areas and recognizes that they can do so profitably using a shared access model and utilizing the channel to market and financing infrastructure of microfinance networks.
The Microfinance Institution	Distribution channel to market. The microfinance partner is a distribution channel and receives ongoing revenue from a share of airtime sales. Additionally, the microfinance institution reaps the benefit of the financing agreement with the Village Phone Operator in terms of interest income. The program can also be used to attract new customers and reward long-standing clients.
Village Phone Company	Revenue for this partner is derived from airtime sales and a revenue sharing model with the other partners. Its goal is to be sustainable and expand the rural reach of telecommunications services
Village Phone Operator	Sells phone airtime for calls to people in their community. Also generates revenue from non-airtime sources such as message delivery, solar charger utilization, etc. The micro-entrepreneurs' other business activities benefit from the Village Phone business. For example, when someone comes to their store to buy a soda, they may make a phone call, or if they come to make a call, they may buy a soda while waiting. Innovative entrepreneurs have created additional adjunct businesses to maximize this 'internal synergy'. One Bangladeshi created a tea house alongside their phone station, and then took it one step further and created a "resting place" (for people to use when waiting for incoming calls) which then evolved into a small hotel. This 'system' of Village Phone Operator activities forms a sustainable livelihood.

In Bangladesh and Uganda, the most important lesson learned is that the model works because everyone is a 'winner'.

- The 'customer': sees an immediate financial return (in terms of opportunity costs) and access to affordable telecommunications services.
- The Village Phone Operator: makes a profit on the margin between their cost and sale price for airtime. The social standing of the Village Phone Operator often increases in their community.
- Telecommunications Company: now reaches customers previously economically inaccessible at a small marginal cost. Although margins are lower, there is a significantly greater volume yielding much greater revenue per phone than 'typical' urban subscribers.
- Microfinance Institution: finds value in the social yield but also in the ongoing revenue stream from credit agreements from Village Phone Operators and from the airtime sales which perpetuate themselves with little additional resources or input.

- The Village Phone Company: covers its costs and generates a surplus in which to extend its mission-driven expansion throughout the country.

At the base of the business pyramid of Village Phone is the Village Phone Operator. The sustainability of their livelihood and their system of businesses is critical to the success of each organization which comprises Village Phone. The following table shows a sample Village Phone Business Analysis – this forms a part of the macro business model.

VILLAGE PHONE OPERATOR BUDGET & SUSTAINABILITY

VPO Daily Revenue	USD
Average VPO margin per minute	$0.10
Average minutes sold per day	20
Total Daily Revenue Net	$2.00

Example MFI Financing	
Equipment Pricing (Loan principal)	$240.00
Loan Term (weeks)	26
Loan Periodicity (weeks)	2
Interest Rate (Flat, Monthly)	4%
TOTAL DAILY OBLIGATION	$1.64

ANALYSIS	USD
Average VPO Daily Income	$2.00
VPO Daily Financial Obligations	$1.64
(Surplus after loan repayment)	$0.36

Breakeven (During Loan)	
VPO Breakeven Minutes / Day	16.35

Revenue Projection (Post-Loan)	
VPO Revenue Projection	$2.00

The business model is built on the average number of minutes sold per day by each Village Phone Operator – some will sell hours, some just a few minutes. There are Village Phone Operators in Uganda consistently selling more than two hours (120 minutes) per day of airtime. The sustainability model also represents an average. The example breakeven analysis above shows that if a Village Phone Operator is selling less than 16 minutes per day, then they are operating at a deficit while they are within in their 26 week loan repayment period. Because we are dealing with averages, there will be Village Phone Operators operating below this utilization, and there will be those who far exceed this average. The idealistic goal is to have all Village Phone Operators operating profitably when we consider their Village Phone business as stand-alone.

For those Village Phone Operators operating below the breakeven utilization, we should not consider this non-sustainable or a business failure, nor should we consider this Village Phone Business a burden driving the poor entrepreneur further into poverty. We are working with a system which holistically provides for a sustainable livelihood for the Village Phone Operator and their family. Village Phone Operators are selected by their communities and by their member microfinance institutions as upstanding and respected citizens who have proven their entrepreneurial skills and have established a record of success in their micro-entrepreneurial activities. Their ongoing relationship with the microfinance institution is based upon a solid credit record. The basis of success of the Village Phone Operator business must be considered as a part of the whole, 'internally synergistic livelihood' as discussed in the table above. In this context, it is important to note that after the loan is repaid, the Village Phone Operator's gross revenue is money straight to their family revenue.

There is often a synergistic relationship between the Village Phone Operator's "phone business" and their "primary business". For example, an operator who runs a small shop selling soft drinks will sell drinks to people who come to use the phone. This increase in revenue for the "primary business" can make the phone endeavor profitable even for those operating below breakeven utilization.

In Bangladesh, Village Phone Operators are offered an eight week 'commissioning period' where they essentially trial the business and make sure that it works for them and their community. A negligible percentage of Village Phone Operators decide not to pursue this business beyond the commissioning period. There are complex formulas for determining the profit sharing during the commissioning period and challenges as to ownership and actual transfer of ownership. After extensive consultation with the sector and a pilot test in Uganda, it was determined that the commissioning period was not necessary and loan obligations and transfer of ownership and responsibility begin at deployment at the time of signing the Village Phone Operator and loan agreements.

The microfinance institution manual template in *Appendix C* describes the various parameters of designing an appropriate loan package for the Village Phone product.

One of the more challenging areas in the creation of a business model is the formulation of a tariff structure for Village Phone. This is probably the most critical element of negotiations with the Telecommunications Operator partner. There are multiple facets to this dialogue:

MTN	400/=
UTL	450/=
Mango	450/=
Celtel	600/=
East Africa	1200/=
International from	2500/=

- The Village Phone Operator financial analysis should provide an idea of the quantum of net revenue required by a Village Phone Operator in order to sustain their business. Usage assumptions must be created to provide margin per minute figure. This is the starting point – if the Village Phone Operator cannot run a business around their breakeven point (during their loan repayment period) then it will be very challenging to make the Village Phone model work as a whole.

- The structure of the tariff plan should be as simple as possible with as few variables as possible. Peak rates, off-peak rates, discount rates along with destination, network used and destination number provide too many variables when all their combinations are considered. In Uganda, we use six tariffs and the only variable was destination (network or geographic). The rates charged to customers by Village Phone Operators do not change based on time of day. That said, simplicity is not a hard requirement. The

Bangladeshi Village Phone program has a manual, distributed to all Village Phone Operators, which contains four pages of detailed tariff variations.

- The business model will consider all tariff variations and may use a weighted average (blended) tariff to simplify planning, budgeting and analysis. This weighted average tariff (and its breakdown into component costs and allocations) is usually based upon historic usage patterns for subscribers. It is important to note that Village Phone subscribers and their community of customers will not necessarily be represented well by referencing historic calling patterns of a predominantly urban subscriber base. However, at commencement, these 'typical' subscribers may be the only reference point and until the Village Phone business has established enough of a historical record of its own, these will suffice for planning. For example, in Bangladesh there is a large expatriate community (Bangladeshi people who choose to work out of the country), largely drawn from rural communities. Village Phone Operators' calling patterns show a higher percentage of international calls than do GrameenPhone subscribers found in Dhaka.

- Already established channels to market and the comparable tariff structures for these: The Telecommunications Operator may not wish to create anomalies in the positioning and structure of their products as seen by the distribution network. It may be that the tariff structure is defined by existing products – even though those products may serve different market niches, constituencies, or even geographic areas.

- The tariff plans of any competition will have a large part to play in the determination of an appropriate Village Phone tariff structure.

- Government Regulation and Oversight
  - Regulated interconnect rates between local networks and international gateways
  - Regulated wholesale tariffs
  - Excise Taxes

- Universal Access Fund fees / taxes / surcharges

- Unitization and which party benefits from the unitization. For example, if the Telecom Operator sells wholesale in units which are 6 seconds, and the Village Phone Operator sells retail in units of one minute, the Village Phone Operator has the potential to benefit greatly – on average, earning an additional 5 units of retail revenue for each call made.

Hypothetical Tariff Plan

	Note	Qty		Variable	Calculation
Village Phone Subscriber minutes per day			20		
Periodic Service / Connection Fee	1		$0.00		
Unit allocation of Tariff	2		1 min		
Retail	3		$0.20	a	
Wholesale (Incl VAT)			$0.13	b	
VAT (Value Added Tax)		15%	$0.02	c	b / (1 + 15%)
Distribution Channel Comission	4	5%	$0.01	d	(b - c) x 5%
Wholesale (Excluding VAT)			$0.11	e	b - c - d
Village Phone Operator Margin			$0.07	f	a - b
Telecom Operator and Village Phone Company	1,5		$0.11	g	e
APRU			$120.00		g x k x 30

Note 1: A periodic service fee may be required for all subscribers to maintain connection to the network and to avoid phone number being recycled when the phone remains unused for a period of time. In Uganda this was waived for Village Phone

Note 2 : This example assumes a unit is 60 seconds

Note 3 : This Tariff plan is for a single call type (or the weighted average / blended). Variants include allowances for peak, off-peak, Discount, Other Networks, etc...

Note 4 : This percentage allocation is paid to the MFI for their function as the Distribution Channel - This percentage is negotiated with the Telecom Operator and should be consistent with usual distribution channel commissions

Note 5 : Excise taxation, Universal Access Fund, Interconnect fees, Amortization of infrastructure investment, profit, and other incidental 'external' 'charges' are paid from this amount

The business model and financial projections form the core of the Business Plan for the proposed venture.

STEPS FOR REPLICATION – 3: IDENTIFY STAKEHOLDERS AND RELATIONSHIPS

Multiple stakeholders need to come together for the Village Phone program, each with specific roles and responsibilities.

Initial Catalyst / Champion

The effort must initially be conceived and driven by an individual or organization to bring the concept before the stakeholders. This provides the catalytic action necessary to launch a Village Phone initiative. Such a person could be within a Telecommunications Company, a telecommunications service organization, a microfinance institution, an Non-Governmental Organization (as was the case with Grameen Foundation USA in Uganda), or an individual entrepreneur. The catalyst will typically forge partnerships with the microfinance institutions and the Telecommunications Company. The catalyst may evolve into the Village Phone Company / Entity / Department over time as the initiative gains momentum and a form of its own.

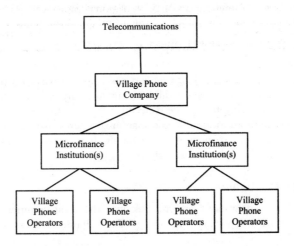

Village Phone Company

The Village Phone company brings all the parties together and serves to "carry the torch" for the Village Phone effort. It is responsible for:

- Further forging and maintaining of partnerships with telecommunication company and microfinance institutions
- Strategic planning
- Program monitoring, evaluation, and reporting
- Manage general problem solving
- Training of microfinance institution staff

- Consolidate and disseminate knowledge
- Local marketing

It is not a requirement for this role to be played by a separate company – although this is how the programs have been structured in Bangladesh and Uganda. For example, this role could be played by a team within an existing telecommunications company.

Telecommunications Company

The Telecommunications Company provides access to their existing telecommunication infrastructure. In addition, their role is to:

- Validate communications services to rural areas
- Determine tariff structure for Village Phone Operators
- Source, stock and resell all equipment
- Sell prepaid airtime cards (market-specific)
- Provide usage data to Village Phone Company
- Ensure government licensing & regulation compliance
- Facilitate "help line" centre for Village Phone Operators
- Strategic planning with partners

Careful consideration should be given to the Telecom Company which will have established distribution channels for its services. The introduction of an additional channel to market – even though it will be complimentary and not competitive – has the potential to be disruptive. The Telecom Operator may have concerns about certain operational modalities, tariff and margin structures that may be perceived by its existing distribution partners as being unfair or promoting a non-level playing field. These should be addressed as early as possible.

Microfinance Institutions

The Microfinance Institutions are the link into the rural communities, providing access to credit to their clients for starting Village Phone businesses. Their role in the Village Phone program is:

- Process Village Phone Operator selection, applications and appointments
- Finance credit to Village Phone Operators for purchase of phone and starter kits
- Act as conduit for equipment and airtime cards to Village Phone Operators
- Provide access for channel to market
- Undertake strategic planning with partners
- Provide customer support and problem solving for Village Phone Operators
- Monitor appropriate use of phones and airtime
- Monitor, evaluate and report Village Phone Operator performance

The maturity of the microfinance sector will also play a role, as will the extent of regulation of both the microfinance and telecommunications sectors.

Village Phone Operators

Although the Village Phone Operators are the last group to become involved in the program, they too have specific obligations:

- Provide communications service to the community using Village Phone approved tariffs
- Maintain equipment
- Market their business
- Manage user billing and payment collection

The stakeholder structure outlined above is but one of many options available and each replication will likely take a new form. Matters of institutional vision, organizational structure, governance, and ownership will need to be addressed on a country-by-country basis.

Partnership Considerations

Perhaps one reason why the partnership came together between Grameen Foundation and MTN Uganda was that Grameen Foundation made it very clear that ownership and control in the long term were not key objectives – we were offering our services, expertise and corresponding resources and a risk-sharing partnership to create a new market and a new distribution channel for MTN Uganda – we could also point to the success of Village Phone in Bangladesh as established by Grameen Telecom. Our motives were social and not threatening to MTN Uganda, but MTN recognized that Grameen Foundation approached this social objective with a clear sense of the business approach required to make it sustainable, successful, and profitable. There was an advantage to Grameen Foundation being an NGO in building the partnership with MTN Uganda. Corporate entities, consulting groups or Telecom Service Providers who work to forge Village Phone partnerships will meet challenges that Grameen Foundation did not have to face.

A wide array of partnerships needs to be forged and structured for the Village Phone program to be successful. For the long-term success of the program, it is important for all parties to share the same goals and objectives. These should be addressed and articulated early in the partnership discussions.

Sharing a Vision

It is of the utmost importance that all potential partners share a vision with respect to Village Phone. While all motivations may not be consistent, they can at least be complementary and the synergy brought through the common vision can build an incredibly strong partnership. Each partner will bring a unique skill set, infrastructure, and resources that will contribute to the partnership and define the nature of each party's role.

In the context of partnership discussions, questions should be posed to get to the essence of these issues:

- What is each partner's commitment to a social mission?
- How important is the financial bottom-line for the business vs. the public relations / Corporate Social Responsibility 'value' of serving the rural poor?
- To what extent is the Telecommunication Operator prepared to integrate the microfinance sector as a legitimate distribution 'channel to market', recognizing that there may have to be unique aspects to this distribution relationship?
- Do all parties have a commitment to sustainable operations – are microfinance institutions operating using 'Best Practices' methodologies, what are their respective positions on subsidies?
- Do all partners agree on a geographic focus (rural vs. urban)?
- Is there agreement as to the target market niche – are the poorest rural villagers exclusively targeted to be Village Phone Operators, or what is the percentage of total Village Phone Operators that should be in this category? Is this even a shared concern?
- What are acceptable return-on-investment and internal-rate-of-return (ROI / IRR) rates for the Telecommunications Operator as they consider their investment – are these the same yardsticks used to evaluate other business opportunities? (perhaps there is an intangible mixed into their thinking as they consider the un-quantifiable value of additional public relations and 'recognition' with the Government)
- The answer to this question will guide many future decisions:
  - The *primary* reasons for the Telecom Operator to partner to launch Village Phone are:
    - Corporate Social Responsibility
    - Government regulatory or licensing requirements
    - It is good business

Formalizing the Partnerships

Following discussions and verbal agreements in principal, the agreement should be documented and formalized, if only in an non-binding Memorandum of Understanding (MOU) or Letter of Intent (LOI). A Non-Disclosure Agreement (NDA) will usually be required also. More legal forms of these agreement should follow later in the process.

STEPS FOR REPLICATION – 4: STRUCTURING THE COMPANY

Once the basic partnerships have been established, a formal infrastructure needs to be put in place to create a Village Phone initiative. In Bangladesh and Uganda, a separate company was created to "carry the flame" for Village Phone. When MTN villagePhone was founded in Uganda, there were a number of structural issues that were taken into consideration.

Low cost infrastructure

Long-term sustainability is one of the primary objectives of the Village Phone program. Sustainability is an enabling element - it is only if the program exists over an extended time that it can achieve its mission. An important piece in the sustainability equation is the on-going costs of the Village Phone Company. Every effort should be made to keep the infrastructure costs as low as possible.

For example, local staff and management should always be hired for the Village Phone Company. Village Phone in Uganda is not structured to support expatriate salaries and benefit packages. Local staff bring other advantages too, such as language skills and connections with the communities. More fundamentally, local management and staff ensure that the operations of the company are consistent with local modes and norms and that foreign NGOs are not going to impose Western values and models on an environment for which these are not appropriate.

It is also possible to lower costs by outsourcing some functions, such as accounting, information technology support, human resources, and marketing. MTN villagePhone operates with a staff of just five people (a manager, three field officers, and an administrative assistant) by outsourcing these functions to MTN Uganda who performs them in exchange for a monthly fee.

A part of developing a low cost infrastructure is developing a structured growth plan. Uganda contains fifty-six districts – in order to efficiently use resources, prudent planning would suggest a phased approach, grouping districts into regions and addressing the market rollout regionally. This approach has advantages:

- minimizes travel times between meetings, deployments, trainings
- increases focus and improves the quality of the offering
- creates opportunities for larger training groups, bringing more people together at a time and avoids having to lead multiple, independent trainings
- monitoring becomes easier
- Village Phone Operator and microfinance institution support is easier
- operational changes are easier to implement, especially in the early phases of the program

An active, engaged and knowledgeable Board of Directors is also a critical factor in allowing the company to operate on a thin infrastructure.

For-Profit, Not-For-Profit or Not-for-Loss

Before creating a new company in Uganda to manage the Village Phone program, there was considerable discussion about whether this company should be structured as a "for-profit" or "not for profit" organization. For Grameen Foundation, this was not so much a philosophical question as a practical one. What legal entity would allow us to come together with MTN Uganda in a partnership we had conceptually described with the social and financial goals elaborated in our 'Heads of Agreement'? In Uganda, this legal structure dictated that we form MTN villagePhone as a Corporation registered under the Laws and statues of Uganda - a for-profit entity. Grameen Foundation chooses to view this not as dictating the goal of the company, but merely as a necessary tool to fulfill our social mission. Grameen Foundation's 501c(3) status in the USA is not impacted by being shareholders in this entity – an important consideration for any initiative and organization considering corporate structure and ownership issues.

Corporate Social Responsibility

Many large corporations feel that they have an obligation to reach out and fulfill a social need beyond their core business. Village Phone could be considered as such a venture. It is directly aligned with MTN Uganda's core business, but at the same time does indeed satisfy a great social need. Grameen Foundation did not engage MTN Uganda on the basis that it was their social obligation to participate in this program. Instead, Grameen Foundation engaged MTN Uganda on the basis that this opportunity made good business sense. The positive public relations that results is merely a bonus.

Ownership and Governance

It is important to determine who will own the Village Phone Company and who will govern and guide its strategic direction. MTN villagePhone in Uganda is a joint venture company newly created and is owned equally by Grameen Foundation USA and MTN Uganda. MTN villagePhone's board of directors is comprised of two representatives from each of these foundation organizations as well as one independent Ugandan representative. Issues such as foreign ownership, directors' liability, Foreign Corrupt Practices Act (USA), and dividend policy should be considered.

A shareholders agreement was created between Grameen Foundation and MTN Uganda which outlines the relationship between the parties in extensive detail. This complex legal document was not the starting point for discussion. In order to avoid being slowed by legal jargon, a 'Heads of Agreement' (a.k.a. Memorandum of Understanding) was first developed. In plain English, it details the agreement between the parties This document was then given to legal teams to develop a formal Shareholders Agreement which went before the respective boards of MTN Uganda and Grameen Foundation.

Early in the process, the question was asked if it was possible or advisable to include microfinance institutions as part of the ownership and governance structures of the

Village Phone Company. This concept held allure for Grameen Foundation as the organizational culture and modus operandi is to be inclusive and to push ownership to the grassroots. Many factors were considered in this debate, as well as consultations with MTN Uganda. The corporate sector has not typically interacted with the Non-Governmental Organization (NGO) sector and they often find little common ground, with different corporate cultures, missions, visions, and financial requirements. The intermediary organization – The Village Phone Company – was created to build a bridge between these two cultures. Diversity on a board of directors is a good thing but it presupposes that the fundamentals are agreed and it may be challenging in many instances to include both the microfinance institution sector and the telecommunications operator on the board. One additional factor to consider is the number of owners – how many shareholders and constituents would be reasonable and how to draw lines which are defensible, consistent and fair. The size of the board itself was also a related consideration. Where many microfinance institutions are not of sufficient liquidity (as is most often the case), the question of what actually would comprise the shareholders equity contribution must be asked. Microfinance institutions being NGOs would not typically have liquidity, or a mission-driven mandate to become shareholders in a corporate entity, which may be a for-profit entity. This question also raises governance issues for NGOs.

Having said this, it will always be possible for a replicator to structure a Village Phone Company in any way they choose (within the confines of local law). There are no fundamental barriers to microfinance institutions participating in the ownership and governance structures.

It has also been debated if the Village Phone Operators themselves should become shareholding partners. The Grameen Bank in Bangladesh is owned in majority by its 3.8 million members. These members are represented on the board of the Grameen Bank by elected representatives from the membership. There is every reason to believe that a similar structure could be conceived for a Village Phone Company. The challenge in Uganda is that Village Phone Company really has no operational relationship to the Village Phone Operator – all interfaces are through the microfinance institution. It may complicate the relationship and delineation of roles and responsibilities if the Village Phone Operators become owners in a company that engages their 'parent organization' (the microfinance institution) in another relationship. Again, this could be done and many challenges would have to be worked through – challenges which we chose not to take on in Uganda. We encourage others to explore this further.

Microfinance Institutions

The microfinance sector cannot be seen as a homogeneous distribution channel. It can be convenient to view the sector as a whole as the 'channel to ,market' for the Village Phone methodology, but in reality, it consists of many individual microfinance institutions which differ in many ways:

- Social mission
- Management style
- Governance, ownership, network affiliation
- 'Corporate' structure
- Sectarian / non-sectarian
- Balance between social and financial goals
- Credit policies
- Operational lending methodologies
- Age and maturity (self sufficiency and outreach)
- Efficiency and performance (PAR, OER)
- Financing coalition in support of operations and growth
- Credit 'Plus' (Education, Health, BDS, Insurances, etc.)
- Cash and security policies
- Financial liquidity (and ratios, e.g. Institutional Debt to Outstanding portfolio)
- Lending
  - Loan size
  - Loan term and periodicity
  - Interest Rates (Comparing "apples to apples" –Effective Interest Rates – SEEP Definitions)
  - Methodology
    - Grameen-style solidarity groups and centers
    - Village banking
    - Individual
    - Formal bank
    - Credit Union
- National affiliation with an Association or Forum of Microfinance Institutions
- Gender policy
- Poverty targeting policy
- Client acquisition methodology

Each organization must be engaged in a manner consistent with their internal goals. Certain adjustments may have to be accommodated by the microfinance institution, and on a macro (national) basis, the Village Phone model will have to be adapted for the environment, culture, and microfinance sector as a whole. We would caution against creating specific accommodations or deals on methodological, operational or financial issues with individual microfinance institutions. The product offered and structure of the relationship between a microfinance institution and the Village

Phone Company must be seen to be consistent across the sector. Within specific microfinance institutions, there may be variations, such as different loan products for clients. These internal differences are necessary and appropriate. In general, the Village Phone Model has been designed to be flexible in order to accommodate as wide a variety of microfinance institution modalities as possible without affecting fundamentals across the sector.

Very early in discussions with microfinance institutions, we presented a "Roles and Responsibilities" diagram so that we could be very clear about mutual expectations and deliverables. These were often watershed moments where partnerships were cemented in clarity and a foundation laid from which to quickly move forward. At this time we often presented a Memorandum of Understanding, a short, clear, one-page document which outlined these roles and responsibilities and sought confirmation of acceptance of these mutual terms. This Memorandum of Understanding is presented as a template (to be customized and localized) as *Appendix B* in this manual.

Pre-Paid vs. Post-Paid

The most fundamental difference between the Village Phone programs in Bangladesh and Uganda is the billing model. In Bangladesh, Grameen Telecom uses a post-paid billing model, generating a bill for each Village Phone Operator at the end of the month that itemizes their calls. This bill is passed on to the Village Phone Operator by Grameen Bank, which is responsible for collecting the monies due.

In Uganda, all of the Village Phone Operators use pre-paid airtime cards. The cards are purchased directly from the microfinance institutions. The prepaid model has advantages and disadvantages. The most significant advantage is vastly reduced operational costs for the Village Phone company as individual billing statements do not need to be prepared and receipts do not need to be tracked. The primary disadvantage is the Village Phone Operators in Uganda must manage their cash flow so that they have enough funds on hand to purchase subsequent airtime cards and to do so before exhausting their current airtime card. To mitigate this risk, MTN villagePhone runs a report every week that indicates the remaining airtime balance for every Village Phone Operator. Those with low airtime balances are proactively contacted by their microfinance institution.

STEPS FOR REPLICATION – 5: FINANCING VILLAGE PHONE

A detailed business plan was created for MTN villagePhone that presented a five-year picture of income and expenses for the company. As the two shareholders, MTN-Uganda and Grameen Foundation USA contributed equal amounts of cash to the company to cover operational costs until the company revenues exceeded expenses in the third year of operations.

Each organization or individual who wishes to replicate the Village Phone model will have to approach the financing and funding question in their own way.

Village Phone could be considered as a good investment and the business plan in Uganda shows strong financials. However, it is an investment not without risks. Political stability and currency fluctuations can have profound impact, and the business model is built upon many exogenous variables. Innovative and socially-oriented venture capital may fund a Village Phone initiative in the future.

Many of the steps that are described in this replication regimen occur prior to the launch of business. Traditional investment thinking would consider these pre-incorporation costs as not relevant to the ongoing investment opportunity. However, as with any holistic funding strategy, there must be recognition of the costs incurred in getting the opportunity 'investment ready'. The investment should recognize the early-stage contributions and contributors in its structure.

Being an NGO, Grameen Foundation sought support for its Village Phone project from a broad constituency including private philanthropists, multilateral and bilateral development organizations. These individuals and organizations are listed at the start of this manual and we acknowledge and honor their confidence in Grameen Foundation, the Village Phone initiative in Uganda and the global movement that it can spawn.

STEPS FOR REPLICATION – 6: ESTABLISH OPERATIONAL FOUNDATION

It is important to establish a strong operational foundation for the Village Phone business. Village Phone is a business with responsibilities to its investors, shareholders, and partners as well as the end users who will come to rely upon the communications services offered through the community of thousands of Village Phone Operators. It is not prudent operating practice, therefore, to make it up as you go along. Creation and documentation of detailed procedures is essential for smooth operations.

Grameen has developed detailed "Operations Manuals" in both Bangladesh and Uganda. The Operations Manual should describe the company processes, procedures and the framework for all operations. Grameen Foundation considers this document "institutional knowledge'" and it is an essential tool for training new employees. For example, if a new Managing Director of the Village Phone Company needs to be hired, the Operations Manual will go a long way to induct the new employee into the company, including its history, mission, vision, stakeholders and workflow. It is a living document intended to evolve with the organization and the environment. It is the responsibility of the management team to maintain this document and preserve its integrity. The Operations Manual is highly customized for each country and is proprietary by its very nature in describing the internal operational mechanics of a Village Phone Company and its various interactions.

The Operations Manual is the most environment specific document describing Village Phone and as such Grameen Foundation cannot guide the detail. A general template is provided in Appendix E. The Operations Manual exists with a family of documents which as a whole form both the guideline for replicating the Grameen Village Phone experience and for running a Village Phone business.

The Operations Manuals from Bangladesh and Uganda provide some good examples for the types of detailed processes that were created. The "Program Overview" from Uganda provides a high-level picture of all the parties involved and how they work together:

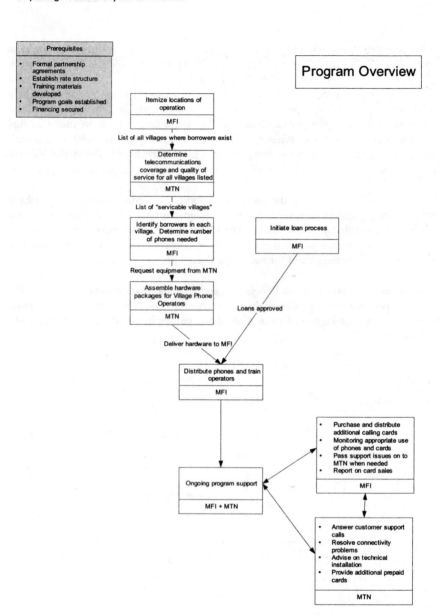

An understanding of the interactions between all constituents helps to ensure that the business runs smoothly. This particular diagram models the partner interactions in Uganda.

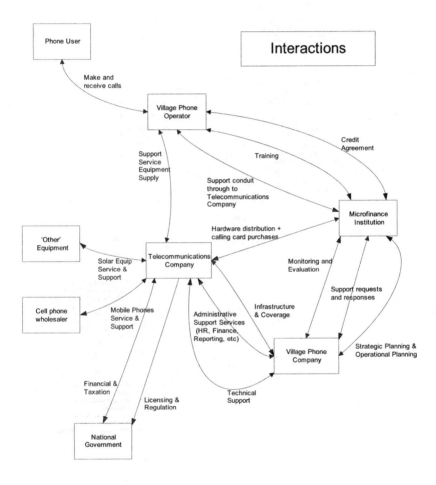

Note that in this representation "Telecommunications Company" is not differentiated – no distinction is made between groups within this company. This is done at a lower level of modeling.

This particular diagram models the partner interactions in Bangladesh:

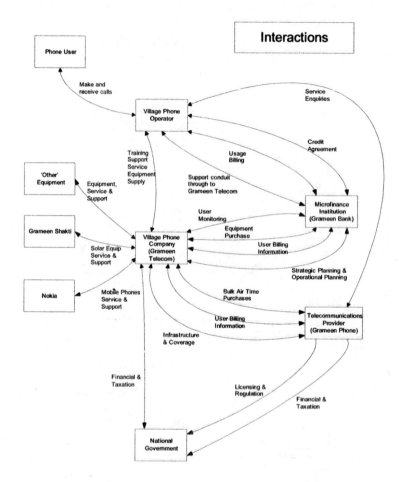

All processes should be modeled. An example for the flow of money for Village Phone in Bangladesh is shown below:

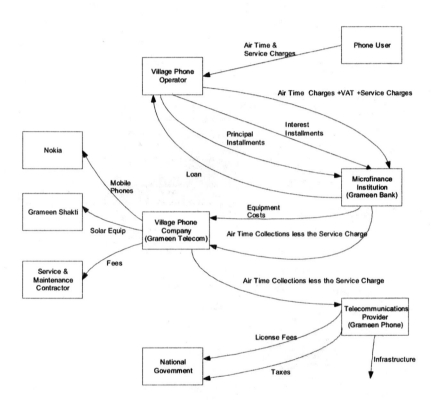

Money Flow

NOTES:

Grameen Bank holds user equipment as collateral
Grameen Telecom is the Nokia Dealer for Bangladesh

Another example of the process modeling necessary to understand the business is shown below. This particular example is the process for the launch of a new Village Phone business in Bangladesh:

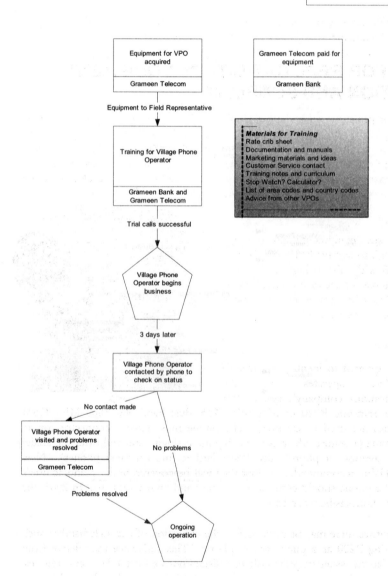

These examples are but a portion of the overall process mapping of the operations of the Village Phone business. Any replicator of the Village Phone model will have to perform a similar analysis and mapping to understand their business, its interactions and external interfaces. Some notes on aspects of the various processes are described below. Not all process stages and interactions are addressed here and further detail is in the microfinance institution manual (*Appendix C*) and the Village Phone Operator manual (*Appendix D*).

The modeling is an iterative process and the model will be dynamic and form a part of the living documentation of the Village Phone business.

STEPS FOR REPLICATION – 7: EQUIPMENT SELECTION AND SOURCING

Before a pilot program can be launched, all of the appropriate equipment must be defined, suppliers identified, and channels established (including defining terms of supply and payment). In addition, the infrastructure for warranty, service and support must be created. These pieces are essential for pricing to be determined (i.e., what it will cost for a Village Phone Operator to start a business) and understanding how to address problems once businesses are created.

In general, the equipment needs to be durable enough to survive heavy use in rural environments while also being affordable to keep the total cost of the loan needed to start the Village Phone business as low as possible – a key to the business model.

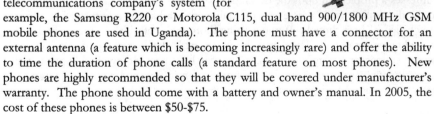

Mobile phone

The first component to identify is a mobile phone that operates on the telecommunications company's system (for example, the Samsung R220 or Motorola C115, dual band 900/1800 MHz GSM mobile phones are used in Uganda). The phone must have a connector for an external antenna (a feature which is becoming increasingly rare) and offer the ability to time the duration of phone calls (a standard feature on most phones). New phones are highly recommended so that they will be covered under manufacturer's warranty. The phone should come with a battery and owner's manual. In 2005, the cost of these phones is between $50-$75.

In some countries there may be resistance to the utilization of a mobile handset such as the Samsung R220 as a public access phone. This resistance may derive from perceived reliability issues or previously established norms for public access phones. Desktop wireless phones provide an option here and these can be obtained from a number of vendors. However, these units are typically more expensive than a mobile handset. This additional cost can cause the sustainability of the business model to collapse, and careful analysis should be done before committing to higher priced phones.

Compatibility with the Telecommunications Operator's network will also be a consideration. While ostensibly all GSM phones are compatible with the worldwide GSM technical standard, many telecommunications operators like to test and validate any phone that will be utilized on their network to ensure it performs to the standard specification, the network specification, and cannot disrupt network timing or frequency bounds.

To aid the business model sustainability, it has been suggested that we engage telephone manufacturers in a relationship which would enable access to telephones at wholesale or subsidized rates. Anecdotally, it is said that manufacturers have significant stocks of non-current model phones and these are in fact a liability (stocking costs). Theoretically, the manufacturers would be happy to provide these to a socially beneficial initiative such as Village Phone. We have not yet been able to engage the manufacturers in any such discussion and encourage others to pursue this discussion. One thing to be aware of in pursuing such a course of action is the need to be careful not to build a business model that is fundamentally reliant upon such corporate good-will – such good-will can be transient and short lived.

In Europe, the United States, and other developed countries, subscribers often upgrade their wireless phone and there are stockpiles of used phones in people's bottom drawers. Many socially oriented initiatives have been launched to recycle these phones and reuse them in the community – potentially providing access for those for whom equipment cost is a barrier to entry. Certainly in the U.S. this approach has not had much impact because telecommunications operators (and even virtual operators) give away new handsets with a new service contract. The equipment cost itself provides no barrier to being a subscriber on a wireless network. Used cell phones continue to accrue and in the future these may even present an environmental concern. Gathering these handsets and recycling them for reuse in the developing world provides an obvious social good. It has the potential to addresses a problem in both the developed world (accrual of 'junk' phones) and also in the developing world where cost of equipment is a barrier to participation. There are challenges here though. Without being thoroughly refurbished, these phones are an unknown quantity. There may be issues with the battery condition, key pad action, connector quality and so on. They may have been dropped and operate only intermittently; they may have been exposed to moisture and so exhibit unwanted behavior in humid environments.

Another significant issue is SIM locking; when a phone is provided as a part of a service contract it is usually electronically locked to that provider so that the purchaser cannot just take the new phone and switch operators.. This lock remains in effect until it is disabled by the originating Network Operator – even on an inactive phone. To make a phone usable on another network, the necessary codes must be obtained and the phone unlocked. For phones of unknown origin, this can be problematic. Obviously, it would be unwise to provide these phones in this unknown state to the poor rural, often technically illiterate Village Phone Operators who would have little recourse and who come to rely upon these devices, not as mere conveniences, but as tools necessary to sustain their livelihood through their Village Phone business.

While recycled phones could be refurbished and fitted with a new battery, repackaged and provided with OEM user manuals, imported into the country of need and then deployed as viable Village Phones, this comes at a cost: gathering the phones from across a wide geographic area, refurbishment, packaging, shipping, customs duties (even on used equipment) and ultimately VAT. These costs can add up and be significant when compared to the cost of a new phone. An additional consideration in this plan is the warranty terms for support of these phones – how would this be done, who would locally represent these phones, how would they be serviced and by whom? U.S.-based GSM networks typically operate on the 1900MHz frequency band and this is atypical – European, Asian and African GSM networks are usually 900 / 1800MHz dual band and unless a tri-band phone is available, a U.S. phone will not work in Africa or Asia. The handsets for CDMA, TDMA or other network protocols used by many US Telecom Operators are generally tightly coupled to their network provider in the U.S. – we have not researched the compatibility and interopera bility of these to any great extent.

In the developing world, there are phones available that are allegedly 'brand name' phones but which are in fact copies. It is a good idea to deal with reputable suppliers and be aware when comparing prices that you may not be comparing "apples with apples".

In Uganda, and also in Bangladesh, the Village Phone handset is standardized to provide the best opportunity for support to the network of Village Phone operators. A limited number of models and brands of phones are much easier to support and for which to provide necessary parts and technical support. In Bangladesh the first phone used was the Nokia 5110. As this became obsolete, a new model was deployed – the next evolution of the 5110. This was a robust phone and its successors also proved to be so. In Uganda we searched for a suitable handset and we initially chose the Samsung R220. Our guiding specification is described:

Wireless Phone Specification

- GSM Network

- Dual Band: 900MHz and 1800MHz

- Connector for an external antenna cable

- Rugged

- No flip, slides, pull-up antennas or other moving parts

- Large clear buttons

- Operating manuals

- In-country warranty, service and support (preferably through an extensive national network)

- SMS capable

- Able to accommodate additional SIM card programming (for Telecom Operator specific menu driven value-added services)

- Call timer built in to phone functionality

- Capable of being charged from a 12V source (e.g. car charger)

- Removable rubber plugs for all external holes in the phone (e.g.,: earpiece, charging, data interface, etc.)

- Battery life - greater than 3 hours 'calling time'

- Battery has no 'memory effect'

- Battery life – greater than two years (daily cycled)

- Cost target – less than US$ 60

Initially we did not provide earpieces with the Village Phone equipment kits as we believed that these would be a fragile component and prone to breakage. After we deployed some kits with the earpiece included, we found that these were used extensively and enabled the Village Phone Operator to "control" the phone even while a customer was making a call. This was apparently important to them. It also reduced strain on the cable connecting the phone to the external antenna.

More recently, as we strive to maximize the value for the Village Phone Operator, we have trialed the Motorola C115 as it costs approximately $30 less than the Samsung R220. This Motorola phone seems robust and appropriate for use as a Village Phone, though it is not able to utilize the functionality on an advanced 32K SIM card which has been programmed to provide additional menus and functionality on the handset. This factor will be a consideration as we tradeoff price against functionality.

External antenna

In order for Village Phones to operate more than 15km from a GSM base station[14], an external antenna is required. This will allow a GSM handset to operate up to 35km away from a base station. To the extent that antennas are not widely utilized, the Village Phone Operator will have a technical competitive advantage and will also bring telecommunications services to areas not previously accessible. The antenna must have Line Of Sight (LOS) to the base station. It will not "boost" network reception where a hill is between the base station and the handset antenna. The antenna should be mounted on a tall pole and the correct orientation must be ensured (usually vertically polarized signal) and the direction of the antenna should be toward the nearest base station. It may be, however, that the strongest signal will not be from the closest base, but from one where the line of sight is not obscured.

The equipment package does not include a pole upon which to mount the antenna, which we recommend should be 10 meters above ground. What usually happens at the deployment of the new Village Phone business is that the entire village community mobilizes and finds a suitable mounting pole (often a local tree or bamboo) and they collectively orient and mount the antenna and secure the pole to the place of business for the Village Phone Operator. This becomes a community celebration. In Rwanda, where significant deforestation has occurred in order to satisfy demand for household fuel, it is illegal to chop down trees. Alternative methods of mounting the antenna will have to be found and this may have an impact upon the business model.

The directional Yagi antenna with 10 meters of coaxial cable must also have an adapter cable to connect it to the phone. The total cost is approximately $30. This short interconnect cable (the "patch cable") joining the coax to the phone is one of the more problematic pieces of equipment in the whole package as it is frequently flexed and is therefore prone to breaking. We have worked with manufacturers to make this more robust. Care must also be taken when connecting the antenna to the telephone. We make a special point to train the Village Phone Operators to not use the connection to the phone as the connect / disconnect point – the disconnect should be at the junction of the patch cable and the 10 meter coax cable.

Some antenna manufacturers supply the antenna with a short (10 cm) 'tail' with a coaxial connector to which the long 10 meter coax cable is connected; others come with the 10 meter coaxial directly coming from the sealed electronics that are a part of the antenna. There are positive and negatives to both of these – the short tail provides an exposed connector to the elements and is a source of failure and yet if a failure does occur, the cable and antenna can be independently replaced as necessary. The cable also does not get stressed during the installation process. With the long cable, there is no exposed external join and the antenna and cable are essentially one unit. This is the simpler solution and as such, preferable.

---

[14] Approximately, and contingent upon base station power, transceiver orientation, weather, terrain, foliage coverage, handset power, Line of sight, reflections, etc.…

Recharging solution

Most Village Phones operate in areas where reliable electricity supply is not available. Operating a business in this environment clearly dictates that a charging solution must be a part of the equipment package. Our initial desire was to provide a solar solution which would make reliance upon any external power unnecessary. We worked with suppliers to provide a solar panel and an adapter which was an after-market cigarette lighter adapter used for charging in a car. With modern battery technology, this direct connection proved to be an unreliable method for charging. Lithium Ion batteries most common on handsets today do not respond well to the fluctuations that result from this solution. In fact, we found that the phone discharged through a dark solar panel. This problem was compounded by the aftermarket car charger, which was not designed specifically for the Samsung phone. These car chargers had problems with internal short circuits, and in some cases it is believed that they caused failure of the phone battery itself. A number of overlapping problems caused us to discard this solution and search for a more robust long-term solar solution. There are a multitude of manufacturers who claim that their solar panels can be connected directly to a phone and that this will charge the phone in a short period of time. This may have been true for the older Nokia phones which had Nickel Cadmium batteries (with the associated memory effect problem), but it is certainly not true for Lithium Ion batteries. These cheap solutions cannot be relied upon to charge a phone when it is cloudy, and this is necessary as these Village Phone businesses must be able to operate independently of the weather.

We currently supply a lead-acid car battery with the equipment package. This will charge the phone for up to two months at which time the Village Phone Operator must take the car battery to a charging station for it to be recharged. In Uganda these are common, as use of car batteries is a regular source of everyday power. A charge can cost as little as $1, which has a small impact on the Village Phone Operator business model once every two months.

Initially we provided an interconnect cable with the car battery with two large alligator clips for the Village Phone Operator to attach to the car battery terminals. We quickly found that this was not a good solution as they clips were often connected backwards and the reverse polarity immediately caused the electronics of the car charger to melt. We switched to Samsung OEM car chargers which have a replaceable fuse and also supplied this charging cable with bolt-on clamp to the car battery posts which could not be removed. We now have a robust, cheap charging solution which works well within the cultural context – it is familiar, serviceable and commonly available.

The Village Phone Operators can and do offer charging as a service to their communities – others often come and use their car battery to charge their own phones, and the Village Phone Operator of course charges for this service.

- Car Battery Solution:
  - cost approximately US$30, including interconnect cable and OEM cigarette charging adapter
- Solar Energy Solution
  - cost approximately US$90, including solar panel, charging electronics and OEM cigarette charging adapter

SIM card and airtime

The value of a Village Phone business could be construed to be in the equipment that is a part of the package, however this is only part of the case. The piece that makes this business viable for the Village Phone Operator is the network connection and their ability to access wholesale airtime rates, which in turn enables them to resell airtime to their community at competitive rates. Without this value, the Village Phone Operator could just buy retail airtime and would then have to mark up the airtime, without the competitive edge over other entrepreneurs working independently outside the Village Phone framework.

Airtime is not specifically created for Village Phone Operators – this is a generic commodity. The benefit for the Village Phone Operator is in the SIM card which allows for a different rate to be applied per unit (minute) in the back-office pre-paid billing platform. The pre-paid account for a Village Phone Operator is debited for a wholesale rate per unit rather than a retail amount. The Village Phone Operator margin is the difference between these two.

The original equipment package for a Village Phone Operator includes a special Village Phone SIM card (for GSM) and also prepaid airtime for 2-3 weeks of operation (value approximately $45).

Marketing collateral

An important early lesson for the Village Phone program in Uganda was the essential role of local marketing. We initially launched the pilot without any marketing collateral provided to the Village Phone Operators. Village Phone Operators received training, guidelines, and templates to enable them to create and launch their own local marketing campaign. As we moved deeper into the pilot program, we determined that the Village Phone Operators needed additional help with their marketing activities, and that a key driver to usage of the service was local awareness. We decided upon a strategy which provided the necessary tools to the Village Phone Operator. This included a roadside sign and a set of business cards which the Village Phone Operator could customize and hand out within their community and to travelers. With this marketing collateral, the Village Phone would quickly become known as a community resource where one could place and receive calls and messages.

The strength of the MTN brand in Uganda is incredible and it is one of, if not the most, recognized brands in Uganda. This brand awareness and strength is an asset to Village Phone and so there is no visibility of Grameen Foundation, Grameen or any hint of foreign involvement in Village Phone – it is Ugandan and is the MTN brand. Consistency of branding and general branding strategy was an element of the business which had to be developed in Uganda and was not derived from the Bangladesh experience. GrameenPhone was the only real player in rural telecommunications in Bangladesh and so the market would assume that a Village Phone was on the GrameenPhone network.

In Bangladesh Village Phone Operators make their own business cards:

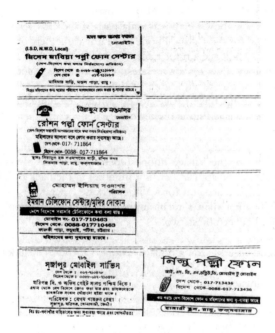

The Bangladeshi Village Phone Operators also make their own roadside signs:

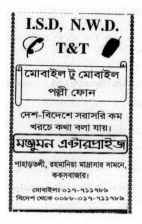

Signage should be suitable for the environment: A simple specification for the roadside sign is shown by way of example. This does not include the mount for the sign and this is an additional consideration. Signs are usually moveable and are brought inside during the night to avoid theft. The mount shown above provides stability in high wind as well as the ability to move it around for security or visibility.

Roadside Sign Considerations (Excluding Mount)	
Color	• How many colors are required? The more colors, the more expensive the sign. *Note: – Branding often requires strict adherence to company colors and it should be validated (by a sample) that the colors required and specified (Pantone equivalents) are representative of what can be achieved by the printing process to be used.*
Sign Size	• Should be large enough to be easily read from 30ft away. In Uganda, the dimensions are 18" x 24".
Mounting Method	• How will the sign be mounted –on a frame? On spikes in the ground, nailed to a wall? • Mounting holes in the sign board: For the design shown above, the following was specified: 13 7/8" between the holes (OD to OD); holes 3/8" down from top of sign to top of hole; left hole 1 13/16" from the left edge; also 1 13/16" for the hole on the right. Hole size is 1/4" (Holes are to be Top and Bottom) - Holes should be resistant to tearing and should have metal, rust proof grommets

continued

Material requirements	<ul><li>UV resistant (Base material as well as printed artwork)</li><li>Fade proof</li><li>Water-proof</li><li>Possibly corrugated plastic</li><li>Mold-proof</li><li>Lifetime expectation (outdoor, tropical locale) - 5 Years</li></ul>
Delivery and Shipping	<ul><li>The materials may or may not be produced locally. For Uganda, it proved to be cheaper to print the roadside sign in Iowa and ship it to Uganda.</li><li>Delivery Date</li><li>Quotation should include shipping</li></ul>
Artwork	<ul><li>Who will provide electronic images (creation of original artwork will cost extra)?</li><li>Proof and Approval Process: specify if you would like to proof and approve the final artwork prior to printing</li></ul>

The Village Phone utilization graph below shows the impact on the deployment of marketing collateral with the Village Phone Operators – a 100% increase in usage can be directly attributed to this marketing material and the associated training that accompanied its deployment. The cost to the Village Phone Operator for this collateral was initially around US$40, an alternate sourcing solution for the roadside sign was found and now costs around $20.

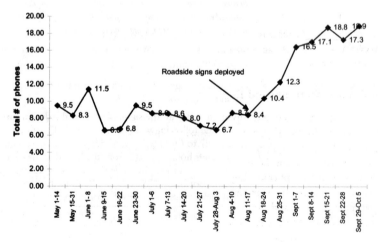

Village Phone utilization showing the impact of marketing collateral during the pilot program

Documentation

In addition to the equipment, the Village Phone Starter kit includes printed documentation to help the Village Phone Operator start the business. A template for the "Manual for Village Phone Operators" can be found in *Appendix D*.

In Rwanda, a very simple two-page "Reference Guide" was developed that summarizes how to perform the most common tasks (making a call, checking airtime balance, loading airtime, checking call duration, reading and sending messages) as well as important things to remember (tips for recharging the phone, how to contact customer support). This guide was printed double-sided on single sheet of paper and then laminated for durability. A sample can be found at the end of *Appendix D*.

In addition to this documentation, some of the equipment will come with its own documentation – the phone handset for example. Power sources such as a solar charging solution may also come with a manual for care and use.

Consideration should be given to the level of literacy that is expected of Village Phone Operators and whether it is a valid assumption that they will be able to read this material and further, whether they can read it in English. Translation of all documentation or a subset of the documentation into local languages should be considered. There are a multitude of languages in Uganda and no common root language to target a translation. Rather than translate the entire documentation set, we summarized the documentation and translated only this. At the time of deployment, the entire documentation set is discussed and the Village Phone Operator can at least know where to go if they need further detail. It is often the case that a literate community member assists the Village Phone Operator on an ongoing basis with documentation understanding and translation.

It is especially useful to develop a list of "frequently used phone numbers" for the Village Phone Operator. This list can include contact information for local government officials, agricultural and veterinary services, health care centers, and local businesses.

Equipment Warranty and Repair

Ongoing maintenance and repair of Village Phone equipment is the responsibility of the Village Phone Operator. Consideration was given to providing used or discounted phone equipment to Village Phone Operators. However, this strategy was rejected in Uganda to give the Village Phone Operators the best possible warranty for the phone they are purchasing. The Manual for Village Phone Operators details the warranty information for each product and procedures for repairing handsets and equipment. More information on warranty and equipment selection is found in the section above that discusses the choice of phone handset.

In both Bangladesh and Uganda, the microfinance institutions ensure that the Village Phone Operator maintains responsibility for their equipment. Only in exceptional circumstances does the microfinance institution contact the Village Phone Company regarding damaged or defective handsets or other equipment. Village Phone Operators are encouraged to call the Village Phone Customer Support Help Line for assistance with hardware problems where they can receive help or, at a minimum, direction to the appropriate support and repair center.

Clear policies vis-à-vis responsibility for equipment, service, and support need to be established and communicated in operational documentation, Supplier, Village Phone Operator and microfinance institution agreements. It is important to minimize the amount of time a Village Phone Operator's business is closed due to equipment problems. One strategy is to maintain a stock of spare parts which can be given to Village Phone Operators while their equipment is being repaired or sourced.

When working with equipment manufacturers, resellers or dealers it will be necessary to negotiate the terms of your supply agreement. Warranty is a necessary element and is not necessarily simple:

- Does the manufacturer have a local agent or does the equipment have to be returned to the manufacturer (who is possibly overseas)?
- What is the turnaround time on a repair?
- Will a local repair shop perform warranty service or does it need to be shipped to another location?
- If shipping / courier is necessary for warranty repair, who bears this cost?
- Can loaner equipment be made available while the unit is being repaired?
- Can the supplier offer an over-supply (3%) in lieu of warranty - this is necessary for equipment where there is no local representation and the cost to ship the equipment back to the manufacturer for repair is more than the replacement cost of the equipment. Failed equipment is simply disposed of and replaced from the oversupply – For example, order 100 antennas from a European-based supplier and receive 103.
- Is the local agent authorized and trained to perform repair – will working with this agent void future warranty claims?

Equipment Procurement and Inventory Management

Policies will have to be established regarding order, reorder, stocking and storage of equipment. This will obviously play a large part in the management of cash flow. It would be prudent to maintain stock levels of at least three months projected deployment, however this guide is based upon the unique environment for Uganda and may differ for other countries depending upon supplier relationships, port processes (import), equipment availability, equipment lead times, shipping modality, invoice process and terms of payment. Each particular environment will determine an appropriate inventory management policy.

There is a fundamental question as to who procures and manages inventory. Related questions are: Who pays? Who assumes the risk for stock? What is an acceptable margin to add for management of inventory? In the case of the Village Phone program in Uganda, this responsibility was agreed to fall under MTN Uganda, as they already had the necessary infrastructure and resources to perform this function. This also aligned well with the goal of minimizing the creation of new infrastructure and reusing existing infrastructure. MTN villagePhone pays MTN Uganda for this outsourced service.

STEPS FOR REPLICATION – 8: DEVELOPING A TRAINING CURRICULUM

Prior to beginning the pilot program, thought needs to be given to training the Village Phone Operators to maximize their ability to establish a strong, viable business. Individual or group training sessions can be held and should be conducted by the microfinance loan officers (who have a relationship with the borrowers) – who themselves will need to be trained prior to starting the pilot.

A sample training agenda is below:

New Village Phone Operator Training Agenda

When a microfinance institution delivers the Village Phone Starter kit to a new Village Phone Operator, a brief 20 minute training session is conducted. Below is an outline for that discussion:

Village Phone Operator Training Outline

At Deployment and Establishment of a NEW Village Phone Business

Introduction
- Welcome and Congratulations
- Why you have been selected to be a Village Phone Operator
- What it means to be a Village Phone Operator (important community resource)
- The obligations of a Village Phone Operator (roles and responsibilities)
- The Village Phone Operator Training Manual

Understanding the Loan
- Loan amount, duration, principal, periodicity, and repayment schedule
- Grace period
- Effective interest rate
- Lending methodology (Group, individual, other)
- Insurance
- Equipment as collateral
- SIM card connection is the property of the Telecom Operator

Equipment
- The Phone (basic operations, care, charging, warranty)
- Recharging the batteries (solar or battery)
- The Antenna (positioning, warranty)

Business Operations
- Financial basis of the Village Phone business
- Tariffs and services
- Margins for Village Phone Operator
- Breakeven (a discussion in concert with the loan product)
- Airtime purchases
- From whom to purchase (only microfinance institution)
- Process for loading airtime onto Village Phone Account (155)
- Monitoring and maintaining Airtime balance
- Record keeping (phone log)

Marketing
- The roadside sign
- Business cards
- Village Phone market niche
- Radio
- Developing a client base

What Happens if.....
- Something happens to the phone or equipment
- Moving
- Selling the business

Operational Tips
- Airtime buffer and bulk purchases
- Using the phone
- Passwords
- Calling the HelpDesk

As the program matures and a body of knowledge has developed about 'best practices' for Village Phone Operators, the Village Phone Company should convene a series of workshops. These should be ongoing and should be a forum for continual learning in a changing environment. Such a forum brings together as many Village Phone Operators as can be convened in one place; they could be from different microfinance institutions or a single institution. Preparation consists of gathering usage data from the Village Phone Operators who will be in attendance and asking Village Phone Operators themselves to share this data with the forum and describe their business – how it works, who comes, what marketing they do – and any number of subjects about their Village Phone business. Such sharing allows other Village Phone Operators to learn about what works and what does not. Microfinance institution staff and loan officers learn alongside Village Phone Operators and the dissemination of best practices becomes propagated actively through future new Village Phone Operator trainings and meetings with other Village Phone Operators.

Such workshop forums have proven extremely valuable in Uganda. Funding such forums is a challenge and should be budgeted as an operational expense for the Village Phone Company.

STEPS FOR REPLICATION – 9: PILOT PROGRAM

The pilot program serves to put all of the pieces into place that are necessary to operate a Village Phone program on an ongoing basis. It also allows for the collection of "real world" data to validate financial and operational assumptions about the program to determine if it should be taken to a larger scale.

The pilot program can also be an extremely valuable recruiting tool when trying to bring new partners into the Village Phone initiative. There is no substitute for showing prospective partners that existing phones are currently in use and operating successfully.

An example pilot phase plan and agreement template is shown in the table below.

Example Village Phone Pilot Phase Plan and Agreement

Village Phone:

Village Phone in "Oregon": Serving the rural communities of Oregon with affordable and accessible telecommunications services utilizing existing Oregonian Telecom infrastructure in a shared access model and microfinance institutions as a channel to market:

Statement of Intent:

Building upon the Memorandum of Understanding, Oregonian Telecom and Grameen Foundation USA propose a Pilot Phase to subject the assumptions made in the Village Phone business model to real world scrutiny. Observations and outcomes of the Pilot Phase will be used to refine the business and operational model and determine the optimal model to launch the business in Oregon.

Pilot Phase Prerequisites

1. MOU in place between Grameen Foundation USA and Oregonian Telecom
2. NDA in Place between Grameen Foundation USA and Oregonian Telecom
3. Business Model (Subject to refinement and ratification following Pilot Phase)
    a. Tariffs
    b. Unitization
    c. Service Fee
    d. Revenue allocation
    e. Deployment and growth targets
    f. Taxation status
4. Heads of Agreement (Subject to refinement and ratification following Pilot Phase)
5. Board approval (Oregonian Telecom and Grameen Foundation) for expenditures associated with this pilot phase
6. An MSISDN number range shall be allocated to Village Phone
7. Technical mechanisms in place to ensure billing and reporting on Village Phones
8. Branding / Naming / Positioning / Logo
9. Oregonian Telecom should create a financial / budgetary category against which necessary expenditures can be billed and captured
10. Agreed Pilot Phase operational model
11. Two microfinance partners signed up for Pilot Phase
12. Suppliers, sources and delivery channels identified for Village Phone Equipment

continued

Pilot Phase

1. Equipment necessary for Pilot shall be sourced and procured beginning November 7 2005

2. Pilot Phase shall begin January 10, 2006 with first deployments of Village Phones

3. Pilot target deployment will be 50 Village Phone businesses

4. Pilot Phase shall end March 31, 2006

5. Business / Product Launch planned for August 1, 2006

6. Pilot Phase will not include an overt marketing campaign but will incorporate roadside signage and business cards for each Village Phone Operator

7. Two microfinance organizations shall be channel partners for the Pilot Phase

8. Daily detailed reports shall be created showing – Call by call and totals

   a. Airtime usage

   b. Destination number

   c. Originating tower

   d. Switched duration

   e. Billed duration

   f. Billed amount

Resources

1. Grameen Foundation USA will provide on-the-ground resources from the start of the Pilot Phase until Launch

2. Grameen Foundation USA will also provide Project Management for this period.

3. Oregonian Telecom will nominate and appoint a person responsible for Oregonian Telecom scope and interface during the course of the Pilot Phase.

4. Oregonian Telecom will identify a person from November 7 2005 within their procurement function to source necessary equipment to be ready for deployment January 10 2006 – the commencement of the Pilot Phase. Grameen Foundation USA will provide known contacts for equipment sources, drawing upon prior sourcing experience.

5. Oregonian Telecom Customer Support Help Line staff will be briefed and trained on Village Phone in the first week of the Pilot Phase

6. Oregonian Telecom shall provide office space and basic office support for the Grameen Foundation USA on-the-ground staff

Costs and Budget

A budget and an agreement of cost sharing for the pilot phase should be elaborated and agreed upon.

There will of course be significant customizations to this plan for each unique environment and partnership structure. Some of the key items elements are:

Set Pilot Parameters

The results of the pilot program may be used to make a "go/no-go" decision about the future of the Village Phone initiative, so it is important to be clear from the beginning what the scope, duration, goals, and criteria for success will be.

In Uganda, the field testing was split into two distinct efforts. The first was a "trial phase" where a very small number of phones (twenty) were deployed. These businesses were used to identify and resolve any issues with the phone equipment and to establish the early operational processes for the program. The second was a "pilot phase" where the focus was shifted to maximizing Village Phone Operator performance to gauge how well they could perform.

Establish reporting mechanism and data analysis system

Every telecommunications operator has a computer billing system to track and charge for calls. This system is an excellent source of data for Village Phones. Extremely detailed reports can be generated that detail exactly how the Village Phones are being used. For example, how many calls have been placed, how long each call lasts, where people are calling, and what time of day the calls are made.

The pilot phase is the perfect time to determine the process for getting regular usage information from the telecommunications company. Reports should be run on a periodic basis (preferably weekly) and used to regularly monitor the health of the business. These reports will an integral part of regular business operations.

At least once a week, performance of the Village Phone Operators and Microfinance Institutions should be reviewed to keep track of the health of the business. A number of reports have proven to be useful in Uganda:

- Average number of billable minutes per day for each Village Phone Operator
- Average number of billable minutes per day for all Village Phone Operators combined
- Total number of Village Phone businesses
- Number of Village Phones deployed vs. deployment targets
- Total number of Village Phone Operators and the average number of billable minutes per day for each Microfinance Institution
- Remaining airtime balance for each Village Phone Operator (this is useful for identifying individuals who are about to run out of pre-paid airtime)
- Base stations used for each Village Phone (useful for understanding usage patterns and where Village Phone Operators are located)
- Revenue for the Village Phone Company vs. planned revenue
- Number of incoming calls for each Village Phone and duration (useful for calculating additional revenue opportunities)

Below are a few lines from a sample report from Uganda:

From :- 12/04/2004 To :- 18/04/2004

MSISDN	CALLS	DURATION (seconds)	CHARGED DURATION (sec.)	AVG MIN/ DAY	CHARGE	DISTRICT
25639940012	162	10348	15300	36.43	xxxx	Masindi
25639940014	98	5771	9180	21.14	xxxx	Masindi

The primary metric which is monitored is Average Charged Minutes of Use per Day. Every week, reports are given to each Microfinance Institution so they are able to monitor the performance of their Village Phone Operators.

Create Customer Support Help Line

A single point of contact should be established for Village Phone Operators to call if they have problems or questions about using their phone. This should be a different channel than customer support for "regular" customers of the telecommunications company as Village Phone Operators will have unique issues. Tools should be put in place to track issues that Village Phone operators are having so that these can be quickly addressed. *Appendix F* shows a Helpline Reference Manual Template.

Establish MSISDN range

The "MSISDN" (Mobile Station Integrated Services Digital Network) is commonly known as the "phone number" for a mobile phone. This number is defined by the Telecommunications Company and is embedded in the SIM card used on a GSM phone. Working with the Telecommunications Provider, the Village Phone Company should establish a range of MSISDN numbers for the Village Phone program and for each Microfinance Institution partner. All phone numbers that fall within this range will be Village Phones. Room should be left in the definition of the range for future program expansion.

For example, in a country with six digit phone numbers, the following range could be used if 5,000 phones are expected to be deployed with five different microfinance partners:

MSISDN	Microfinance Institution
990000-990999	Partner #1
992000-992999	Partner #2
994000-994999	Partner #3
996000-996999	Partner #4
998000-998999	Partner #5

In this example, the first two digits "99" are used only for Village Phones. Note that room is left between the number ranges to allow for a single partner to expand beyond 1,000 phones and/or for new Microfinance Institution partners to be added over time.

STEPS FOR REPLICATION – 10: OPERATIONALIZE THE BUSINESS

Hire Staff

Following the pilot, original assumptions in the business plan can be replaced with more specific projections. With updated revenue and cost numbers in place, a final staffing plan can be assembled and staff hired.

Few decisions are more important than whom to hire. The success of the Village Phone project is ultimately a function of how strong the individuals are who form the team. The search for staff should continue for as long as it takes to find the right people.

Staff will also be the largest single long-term expense, so it is important to keep the total number of people hired to a minimum and to take the time to find the highest caliber individuals possible. In Uganda, four staff members were hired to start the MTN villagePhone company: a manager, two field officers, and an administrative assistant.

Example Job Description for General Manager

Reports to:

    Board of Directors: Village Phone Company

Core functions:

1. Partner coordination and communication
2. Operations management
3. Strategic planning
4. Market research
5. Financial reporting and analysis
6. Training of microfinance institution staff
7. General problem solving
8. Program monitoring
9. Sourcing and procurement
10. Media coordination
11. Proactive funder contact to shape future RFA/RFP offers
12. Funding proposal development

Major activities

Partner Coordination & Communication

- Initiating regular, proactive communications with partner organizations
- Planning, scheduling, hosting and facilitating Partner strategic planning meetings
- Mediating and drawing partners to consensus
- Ensuring mission focus of the organization
- Coordinating with Telecommunications Operator technical reports of the technical performance of the program

Operations Management

- Innovate new operational strategies
- Responsibility for strategic plan fulfillment - meeting social and economic goals
- Resource recruitment and training

Strategic Planning

- Working with the partners, develop the organizational strategic plan
- Report on plan alignment and fulfillment

Market Research

- Village Phone Company expansion must be based upon solid market research
- Demand research and analysis
- Competition research and understanding of competitive position
- Build an maintain a comprehensive database of market information necessary to make strategic decisions

continued

Financial reporting and analysis

- Propose, review and analyze financial 'deals' to be undertaken by Village Phone Company
- Coordinate legal, corporate, and fiscal assessments of all 'deals'
- Ensure that the Strategic Plan is based upon sound financial principles and the trade-offs are recognized, discussed and documented
- Reporting of fiscal position to the Board

Training of microfinance institution staff

- Training material and curriculum development
- Operating manual translation
- Training of microfinance staff for service delivery

General problem solving

- As referred by the partners
- Direct contact from a Village Phone Operator

Program Monitoring

- Developing a monitoring plan for the organization
- Implementing the monitoring plan
- Analysis and reporting to partner

Sourcing and procurement

- Researching sourcing options for system elements (Mobile phones, antennas, accessories, etc.)
- Supplier negotiation and relationship management
- Inventory management

Media coordination

- Press releases
- Fielding and coordinating all media approached

Proactive funder contact to shape future RFA/RFP offers

- Work proactively with funder organizations to shape future RFA/RFP documents to the strategic requirements of Village Phone Company
- Work with mission staff to inform and gather intelligence regarding local plans, conditions and to 'get in at the ground level' on initiatives, developments and local thinking

Funding proposal development

- Develop and maintain proposal 'boilerplate', material and verbiage
- Drawing upon 'boilerplate' develop dynamic, exciting proposals to funder specifications
- Championing proposals through partner review and approval process
- Delivering approved proposals to the funder organization in a timely manner
- Coordinating all proposal inputs from every corner of the partners and consolidating these into a cohesive selling document.

Additional requirements

Travel

- The General Manager is required to travel to fulfill the requirements of the position. Travel will be within Uganda. Occasional travel to international conferences or to assist in another Village Phone replication may be required.

continued

Personnel specifications

Knowledge and Education

- Masters degree in related field
- Financial analysis
- Microfinance
- International development
- Telecommunications
- Language skills so as to be able to perform within all areas of Uganda
- Spoken and written English is required to a professional level
- Contract negotiation
- Development institutions (DFID, USAID, World Bank, IFC, etc.)

Exposure

- Minimum of ten years of work experience in a relevant field

Example Job Description for Village Phone Field Officer

- Installs, maintains, evaluates, tests and repairs Village Phones and associated equipment in the field and in the workshop.
- Attends to and resolves customer complaints and problem solves.
- Prepares regular reports for the purpose of informing the Manager of problems and challenges encountered and lessons learned, including lack of equipment, tools, spare parts and training required, and makes proposals which could improve working efficiency.
- Supervises, develops and motivates the activities of reporting staff in respect of the activities while remaining "hands on".
- Sets functional strategies and policies.
- Prepares regular reports to the Manager and responds promptly to inquiries and communication from customers, partners, suppliers, etc.
- Informs the Manager immediately of any present or future implications that could result in financial or operational difficulties or losses for the company.
- Identifies own and staff training needs, prepares and implements training plans and provides on-the-job training.
- Organizes and supervises the installation and maintenance of equipment.
- Coordinates delivery schedules and solves technical issues with equipment suppliers.
- Coordinates relevant activities with operators and microfinance institutions.
- Ensures proper housekeeping in the area under his/her jurisdiction.
- Ensures that the function is actively involved in the search for new sites and the sales of payphones.
- Ensures that technical staff are motivated and duly remunerated for all the duties they perform.
- Perform any other relevant duties as may be assigned from time to time.

Ongoing Strategic Planning Process

The initial business planning is probably the most comprehensive, strategic planning process that the organization will ever do. However, ongoing strategic planning is important to the business as it strives to remain relevant and profitable over time in an environment that is ever changing – competition, regulations, maturity, infrastructure updates, changes in technology and so many other elements of the business. A periodic evaluation and forward planning is necessary. Such activity should be planned for and such 'proactive reflective assessment and correction' should be a part of the culture imbued within the organization.

Network Planning

A process for planning growth of the Village Phone network of operators in coordination with the growth of the network infrastructure should be devised. The Telecommunications Operator has vast market experience and this should be valued as the Village Phone Company looks at expansion of its subscriber base. Signal coverage maps from the Telecommunications Operator can be very helpful in developing deployment strategies. The Village Phone Company adds value to the planning process of the Telecommunications Operator by highlighting areas where there is significant demand for telecommunications. Investment decisions for additional infrastructure deployment by the Telecommunications Operator will now include a factor that looks at network traffic (outgoing and incoming calls) that will derive from Village Phones.

Deployment Planning and Forecasting

In order to appropriately manage the business, close cooperation with the channel to market is required. Awareness of the microfinance institution's availability of capital, their capacity in terms of training and resources availability is critical to growing the business in a planned manner. A deployment planning and coordination process is required. This may mean a monthly meeting between management of the microfinance institution and the Manager of the Village Phone Company to review progress, address issues and to look forward to deployment plans for the next month, and quarter. A pro-forma could be created to facilitate this process and this would form a part of the Operations Manual.

Josephine Namala owns a small retail shop in the remote village of Lukonda in the Kayunga district. Before she began operating her Village Phone business, people in her community had to walk over 5km to make a phone call. In the evenings, large groups of people gather in front of her store with their FM radios to listen call-in radio shows. Inside her shop, a large pink sign is posted with the phone numbers for all of the radio stations. The villagers regularly use her village phone to call the radio stations and make their opinions heard nationally.

Village Phone Operators Application and Approval Process

A fundamental of the Village Phone model is in the autonomy that each partner has in determining how their part of the model will operate – the microfinance institutions create the loan product and determine the best way to select Village

Phone Operators. It is interesting to note that different microfinance institutions approach this differently in Uganda. One in particular uses the Village Phone product to attract new entrepreneurs to their institution – it is a marketing product this microfinance institution uses to differentiate themselves from other microfinance institutions and banking alternatives. Other microfinance institutions, in fact the majority of them, use Village Phone to 'reward' loyal and outstanding clients / members for their continued association. In this context, Village Phone Operators are chosen from those members who have been with the microfinance institution the longest and have the best record of repayment.

However the microfinance institution chooses to select and finance their Village Phone Operators, they all deal with a common process in their interactions with the Village Phone Company, and this process will have to be defined. Based upon our experience, we suggest Microfinance Institutions document a set of selection criteria for Village Phone Operators and also define a process for selection. The following can be used as a guideline:

- Regular attendance at peer lending meetings
- High status within the group
- MFI member for at least two years
- 100% repayment history
- Respected as a community member
- Central location for business operations
- Should have an established 'primary' business
- Able to receive telecommunications signal with external antenna
- Overall gender representation consistent with microfinance institution client base

The microfinance institution's role includes the selection of appropriate Village Phone Operators.

However this is done, the microfinance institution and the prospective Village Phone Operator together submit an application to the Village Phone Company for a Village Phone Business. The purpose of this application process is not so much approval of prospective Village Phone Operators put forward, as to initiate a series of events that will result in the establishment of a new Village Phone business. Village Phone Company has no criteria for approval. Trust is placed in the microfinance institution to select and appropriately train the prospective Village Phone Operator such that they will have a successful business. It is, after all, the microfinance institution that holds the credit risk.

Upon receipt of an application process, a series of events must occur:

- Equipment sourcing
- Equipment delivery
- Credit agreements established
- Payment for equipment
- Training
- Number allocation and registration
- Village Phone Operator agreements signed
- Notification of 'Approval' and agreement on a calendar
- 'Bundling' of applications (optional)
- Pricing (the equipment package price may change due to market conditions and currency exchange fluctuations)
- The order process to acquire the necessary equipment forming the 'Starter Kit'

The particular parties / organizations, timing, forms and actions will be unique for each Village Phone program. The process flow should be mapped.

Equipment Order and Acquisition Process for Microfinance Institution

Once a new Village Phone Operator business has been proposed and the process initiated for the establishment of that micro enterprise, the microfinance institution must order the equipment. The order form initiates the process to bring together the elements of the starter kit. A date is agreed and the microfinance institution travels to pick up the equipment from the Distribution Center. Variants on this process may be available where rural Distribution Sub-Centers may disburse equipment, but management of such a distributed system creates a greater management and oversight burden.

The credit policy will have to be created for this transaction and relationship with the microfinance institutions. It may be that a strict cash business policy is implemented.

Call Center – Customer Support Help Line

The network of Village Phone Operators requires support. This can be achieved by tasking the Telecom Operator's call center staff with supporting the Village Phone Operators. Village Phone Operators are no more than a special class of subscriber and as such, no new or additional infrastructure needs to be created to support them. If call center queue lengths and wait times are long, a special priority should be placed on Village Phone Operators – they are generating call volumes significantly higher than a standard subscriber and so the justification for this is easily seen. *Appendix F* contains a reference manual in template form to assist the call center staff in supporting Village Phone Operators. This manual forms the basis of a training session for call center staff. Consideration should be given to whether the call center support should be toll free or charged. Wait times in the call center queue should form a part of this decision criteria. Weekly reports from the call center should provide a framework for analysis of patterns of calling and reasons why a Village Phone Operator would call. These reports, in addition to regular dialogue with staff, are useful in highlighting challenges faced in the field and also trends.

MFI Incentive Program

While a percentage of the revenue for Village Phone is allocated to the microfinance institution, this is institutional revenue – booked by Head Office. Unless the microfinance institution specifically has incentive schemes in place to encourage exceptional performance of their branch and field staff, none of this percentage flows through to those people that are in a position to ensure the success of the Village Phone program – at the grassroots level.

Many microfinance institutions already offer incentives based upon any number of operational performance parameters such as:

- Number of members managed
- Outstanding portfolio
- Portfolio at risk
- New members attracted to the microfinance institution

Incentives are not a significant deviation from this usual practice. Incentives for loan officers or branch staff could be offered based upon:

- Number of Village Phones under management
- Revenues generated through airtime sales to Village Phone Operators under management
- Portfolio at risk for Village Phone Operators
- Average number of minutes sold by Village Phone Operators

An incentive scheme must be culturally appropriate for an microfinance institution – each will have their own standards and practices vis-à-vis incentives offered to branch and field staff. The incentive scheme should be created by the microfinance institution with guidelines offered by the Village Phone Company. An example of such guidelines is provided in the microfinance institution manual template in Appendix C.

This incentive scheme could be an additional percentage offered to the microfinance institutions, or it could come from the amount already offered to the microfinance institution in their role as Distributor.

Administration

The operational focus of the business must be supported by appropriate back-office infrastructure, this includes:

- Finance
  - Accounts receivable
  - Accounts payable
  - Audit
  - Taxation
  - Banking
  - Cash management
  - Budgeting
  - Reporting
- Office space and facilities
- Telecommunications
  - Fax, Phone, Mobile Phone
- Information Technology
  - Company Web Site
  - Email
  - Internet access
  - Server
  - Computers
- Cars and vehicles

Various policies relating to the usual operations of a business also need to be considered:

- Travel policy
- Vehicle use policy
- Communications and press policy

In addition, many forms will have to be created to facilitate appropriate operational visibility and control:

- Order form
- Trip planning report
- Domestic travel requisition
- Field report
- Airtime balances and service fee expirations
- Village Phone Operator call monitoring
- Accountability for loan advance
- Deployment record
- Field visit check list
- Vehicle condition form
- Frequently asked questions about Village Phone
- Staff performance and development review

Human Resources

The people of the Village Phone Company are the most critical asset of the business. They need to be looked after and they need to understand they have an infrastructure that supports them in the performance of their duties. Systems need to be established to ensure prudent policies and appropriate management of:

- Recruitment
- Remuneration and benefits
- Performance management
- Disciplinary code
- Health and medical benefits
- Other benefits
- Staff incentive or bonus schemes

Much of this necessary physical, operational and process infrastructure can be piggy-backed upon those established by the Telecom Operator with these services being outsourced from the Village Phone Company to the Telecom Operator at appropriate charges for such services.

The Operations Manual (See *Appendix E* for a template) provides the framework for Village Phone Company formalization.

Information Technology and Reporting

Knowing what is going on in the business is critical to appropriate and proactive management. Reporting from the various IT systems will greatly enhance operational control of the business. Weekly reports can be defined and created. This is discussed in detail in the Pilot Phase section and should be continued throughout the project.

Capturing information from launch and deployment of Village Phones is required in order to maintain electronic records. This can also provide valuable information as programmatic evaluation is conducted as well as employee compensation packages. This baseline information is important to capture and understand. Often the telecommunications operator systems will not have fields in their database systems to capture such information and so a separate database may need to be created. Care should be taken when considering this as managing parallel systems with replicated (core) data becomes problematic.

Additional Information

Appendix C, the MFI Manual and *Appendix D*, the Reference Manual for Village Phone Operators, contain templates and details of the operational process for the Village Phone business.

STEPS FOR REPLICATION – 11: FORMAL LAUNCH

When all of the pieces of the Village Phone program are in place, a formal marketing event is a great mechanism to generate awareness in the country about the program and recognize the efforts of all of the partners.

The launch event should be appropriate for the country – there is no "one size fits all" solution for introducing Village Phone. In Uganda, an event was held in a rural village about one hour outside of Kampala where a Village Phone operator had a business next to a school. Government officials came to praise the program and make the ceremonial "first call" on the Village Phone. Each of the microfinance partners were present and were able to demonstrate their commitment to the program. Press packets were created that highlighted the background of Village Phone operators from each of the microfinance institutions to bring a "human face" to the story behind Village Phones.

STEPS FOR REPLICATION – 12: MARKETING

The Grameen experience in Uganda highlights the necessity for marketing to educate and inform rural people about the service. Marketing should initially focus on three things:

- Village Phone and its purpose (education, sensitization, awareness)
- Creating demand for microfinance institution partnerships
- Generating interest for individuals to become Village Phone Operators

The stimulation of additional demand focusing on usage of airtime through Village Phone Operators is a later stage of a strategic marketing campaign. The campaign should know what its primary target is and what it is trying to achieve.

Marketing for Village Phone serves two primary constituents: The Village Phone Company and the Telecom Operator. Since Village Phone is likely to build on the strong brand of the Telecom Operator, Village Phone marketing serves the purpose of building and reinforcing brand awareness and also drives additional revenues to the Telecom Operator through greater utilization of existing infrastructure. Marketing budgets need to be developed with this in mind – sources to find a Village Phone marketing campaign should be sought from both the Telecom Operator and the Village Phone Company, and marketing efforts should be coordinated.

Radio is the medium that likely reaches the greatest number of people who are either microfinance institutions, microfinance institution members (prospective Village Phone Operators), or community members who would use such a service if it was to be offered in their village.

Posters placed in microfinance institution offices and handouts distributed at microfinance institution meetings can also be effective, but this can be a costly exercise. Supplements in national newspapers have been used to good effect in Uganda to perform the education and awareness building amongst the population. Recognition of the Village Phone brand in Uganda is now very high – supported by its association with MTN.

There are opportunities for co-branded marketing – with the microfinance institutions or perhaps with equipment suppliers. Such campaigns could benefit everyone. Microfinance institutions leverage their exposure and reputation by being associated with the Telecom Operator's national brand and the Telecom Operator gains credibility amongst the poorest rural communities (a massive new and untapped market) by coming to them with an innovative product that meets their needs within the constraints of their economic environment. Such associations can be leveraged to build strong and effective marketing campaigns.

Road signs, business cards, and t-shirts can be co-branded with both the microfinance institution logo and the Telecom Operator brand.

MTN villagePhone has also printed branded t-shirts and caps which are often worn by the Village Phone Operators – this again creates a strong sense of reliability and the sense that the Village Phone Operator owns and operates a solid business, somewhere a person can go and know they will get a good connection and value for their money.

STEPS FOR REPLICATION – 13: ONGOING OPERATIONS

Identify and resolve problems

An ongoing effort should be made to identify and resolve any problems that the Village Phone Operators are regularly encountering. At least once a month, a meeting should be between the staff of the Village Phone Company and the Customer Support Help Line staff to review the problems that Village Phone Operators are reporting and establish a plan for addressing the highest impact issues. Loan officers at the microfinance institutions who have regular contact with the Village Phone Operators are also a fantastic source of information about problems which need to be addressed.

Document business processes

As the Village Phone program continues and business practices evolve, the Operations Manual which was created during the pilot phase should be regularly updated to reflect new and modified business practices. At some point, there will be staff turnover, and a current document is an essential tool for training new employees.

Appendix E shows a template for an Operations Manual which provides a framework for all details of the operational process, procedures and interfaces for an efficient and effective business. It enables clear transfer of knowledge and ensures a broad understanding of responsibilities. This document is included here in a stripped version, as the environment for which it was developed (MTN villagePhone) is unique and not applicable to any other Village Phone replication except in a broad sense.

Improve efficiency

Every effort should be made to regularly improve the operational efficiency of the Village Phone program. Improvements can be found in a wide range of processes, from procurement of telephone hardware to distribution of phones to loan product design to lending methodology. For example, one microfinance institution in Uganda initiated a program to allow their Village Phone Operators to purchase airtime remotely. They place a phone call to their loan officer who reads the Village Phone Operator the authorization number from the prepaid airtime card and deducts the purchase price from the Operator's account balance. Work is underway to completely automate this process. This has reduced the microfinance institution's cost of delivering pre-paid airtime cards to their Village Phone Operators and eliminated the need for the loan officers to carry pre-paid airtime cards to the field.

STEPS FOR REPLICATION – 14: SHARING BEST PRACTICES

There will inevitably be evolution, localization, and adaptation of Village Phone efforts from country to country. With each implementation, new "best practices" will be created. We encourage all those who catalyze Village Phone projects to contact Grameen Foundation USA and share lessons learned so that Grameen can continue to serve as an international knowledge center for Village Phone best practices, facilitating current and future Village Phone initiatives.

VILLAGE PHONE EVALUATION

Impact Assessment and Evaluation[15]

Documented studies conducted on the Village Phone program in Bangladesh are abundant. However, the context of the MTN villagePhone program differs greatly from the Bangladeshi model; factors ranging from regulatory environment, microfinance institution methodologies employed, telecom infrastructure conditions and cultural and economic conditions all contribute to the variance. Therefore, findings from these studies will have varying degrees of validity in the Ugandan context. As a result, program impact measures have been designed with this local context in mind and allow for programmatic and systemic differences. In addition to using many of the categories for impact assessment outlined in the Bangladesh case studies, this framework explores additional dimensions that may be also significant contributors for positive impact measurement.

Grameen Foundation has conducted preliminary market research that shall enable the development of a monitoring and evaluation framework designed to measure the impact of the Village Phone program. Utilizing this framework, impact will be measured across all entities in the system, from the individual Village Phone Operators to the larger community and to the economy in which they participate. A randomized impact assessment study is currently being planned for a Village Phone program in Rwanda.

One of the key challenges of this research effort is to convert the best available field data (including client data and microfinance institution reports) into useful, usable metrics which can enable trend monitoring, field data-based decision-making, and performance evaluation of the program and the administration of the program. Given the uncertainty and volatility of current and potential reporting mechanisms in this field context, establishing consistent, credible and verifiable parameters for on-going measurement is difficult.

Hypotheses to be tested by the framework

Based upon the findings from research on the Bangladesh model and from anecdotal evidence and informal reports in Uganda, the following are hypotheses for a programmatic evaluation based upon this framework:

1. Village Phone improves the status, mobility and equity of women – both as VP operators and in general, in the broader community.
2. Village Phone improves the status, mobility and equity of the poor: VP operators gain a special designation of importance in the community, they serve wealthier clients and various community members, and VP program distributes access and ownership of technology to the poor.

---

[15] Authorship credit for much of the content of this section goes to Rachel Payne for her work on development of an evaluation framework for Village Phone.

3. Village Phone offers operators and their households a productive, income-generating opportunity that greatly supplements existing household income.
4. Village Phone offers productivity-enhancing, time-saving value for the community it serves and is a marked improvement over alternative communication options.
5. Most Village Phone calls relate to financial, health or social matters and have a positive impact upon the economic stability, well-being and kinship network of the user.

Structuring the framework

In order to ensure that we receive the right information from an evaluation built upon this framework, the framework design is based upon the answers sought from the study and the hypothesis to be tested. The following are factors that require additional information in order to understand more fully how the Village Phone program impacts the rural individuals and communities served:

1. Economic and Financial Impact Measures
2. Health, Well-Being & Environment Measures
3. Education and Advancement Measures
4. Socio-Cultural Impact Measures

Information that we may already know or currently have access to includes the following:

- Microfinance institution client / Village Phone Operator repayment record and credit-worthiness
- Usage statistics
- Distribution and phone density (per population)
- Profit margins and business performance
- Duration of VP ownership

The information sought from this exploratory research covers the following four areas and the associated sub-categories:

1)Economic and Financial Impact Measures

Village Phone Operator

- How clients define and measure financial and economic success
- Amount and percent of household income generated by VP
- Ancillary sales or services resulting from being a Village Phone Operator
- Level of profitability of VP services
- Household member involvement in managing VP services
- Management practices, business performance (success models), conditions impacting profitability

- Poverty level differences: before and after VP ownership (using poverty indicators)
- Asset ownership and investment differences: before and after VP ownership

Community

- How VP affects information asymmetry (enables obtaining market price and foreign exchange information)
- How VP enables new transactions or accelerates previous transactions
- Changes in profitability resulting from access to VP services
- Willingness to pay / Amount of consumer surplus
- Price effects of competition (where present)
- Other economic-related impacts of VP on community:
  - Effect of proximity to VP services (service radius)
  - Effect of type of location of VP services (e.g., market vs. home)
  - Male / Female operator and associated access and reliability effects
  - Uses of discounts

2) Health, Well-Being and Environmental Measures

Village Phone Operator and their Community

- How consumption patterns differ with improved access (& ownership) of VP
- Purpose of use (and associated health-related impacts)
- Type of individuals contacted (and relationship with caller)
- Access to health services and information via VP
- Livestock impacts (information or veterinary service availability)

3) Education and Advancement Measures

Village Phone Operator and their Community

- How being a Village Phone Operator exposes new information/learning; how valued by Village Phone Operator
- Literacy effects in Village Phone Operator household; importance of literacy for Village Phone Operator duties
- How education investment patterns differ with access or ownership of VP

4) Socio-Cultural Impact Measures

Village Phone Operator and their Community

- How being a VPO impacts decision-making within household as a woman
- How being a VPO impacts civic activity within community as a woman
- How being a VPO impacts perception of Village Phone Operator / Village Phone Operator household within community
- How ability to use VPO impacts mobility, business practices and negotiating position within community as a woman
- Type of support structure offered by microfinance institution and VPO group networks

Additional supporting evidence of impact

How does a Village Phone Operator describe "success"?

- "Ability to get meals"
- "To own a house"
- "Have enough clothing"
- "Children can go to school"
- "Can take child to the doctor when sick"
- "The phone is a 'sure' business – a business in a kit"
- "Having a bed to sleep in"

What do Village Phone Operator customers use the phone for?

- Get information about prices (commodities, inputs)
- Handle customer orders or coordinate business activities
- School fees (coordinate, arrange payment)
- Call relatives and friends in other places (e.g. to Kampala from Mbarara)
- Send messages (tell others who has been admitted to hospital)
- Call people for help if encounter trouble on a journey; emergencies, transport
- To call radio station to send announcements (e.g. if there's a death, can call radio station to broadcast a message)
- To stay in touch with family who are no longer nearby
- Wives communicating with husbands who are traveling or in another town (to discuss money, family issues, etc.)
- Call hospital or doctor
- Call police

How does a microfinance institution describe "success"?

- "Growing loan portfolio"
- "(Village Phone Operator) Client's ability to repay loan"
- "Increase employment in community"
- "Build better relationships with customers"
- "Use VP as a marketing tool to attract customers"
- "Get new client/user referrals from Village Phone Operators, those who use phones"
  - Fact that the client got a loan from the microfinance institution to set up their Village Phone Operator makes it better for microfinance institution – community sees it coming from the microfinance institution
  - More clients know about microfinance institution and want a loan from microfinance institution as a result
- "Use VP as a means for communicating with customers"
- "VP can be more appealing than regular loan to customers because loan becomes a direct asset for a business"

How does MTN describe "success"?

- "Village Phone is measured primarily by profit"
  - Cost conscious: low margins mean have to manage revenue
  - Keep staff small; not overburdened with salary costs
  - Work with select local people to build trust and effective marketing
- Wants VP to become a commercial product for entrepreneurs
- Corporate Social Responsibility aspect is quite appealing for MTN potentially

Needs Based Evaluation Framework

Individual Operator	**Primary Needs:** Profitability Sustainability Accessibility	**Impact Category Measure:** Net Income Gain/Increased Household Income Investments in Education Asset Acquisition Ability Investments in Enterprise	**Examples:** Airtime sold (# of minutes) Incremental sales in main business # of kids in school (pre/post) Asset comparison (pre/post) Increased income in main business
Community	**Primary Needs:** Sustainability Accessibility	**Impact Category Measure:** Service Radius/Convenience Demographic diversity Breadth of customers Reliable service Continuous presence	**Examples:** Customer reach (per km/village) Type of clients served/uses Service availability/connectivity Consistent service locations
MTN/ Grameen	**Primary Needs:** Profitability Sustainability Accessibility	**Impact Category Measure:** Net income gain/profit margin Usage & teledensity of service Low-cost service provision Ability to replicate elsewhere	**Examples:** Break-even/Net income positive Airtime sold (# of minutes) Lower costs of deployment, maintenance, support Consistent service locations
MFI	**Primary Needs:** Profitability Sustainability Accessibility	**Impact Category Measure:** Net income gain/profit margin Repayment rate for VP loan Customer acquisition Asset acquisition	**Examples:** Net income positive for VPO loans Airtime sold (# of minutes) via MFI Lower costs of deployment, maintenance, support

Economic & Financial Impact

VPO	Community	MFI	MTN
Perception of success	Access to information (trade & inputs, market prices)	# of clients who are VPOs (# of businesses created/deployed)	# VPO business created/deployed

Profitability of VP business (ROI, return on time effort)	Access to business management services (receive order, call customer)	Increase portfolio outstanding for Village Phone loans	
% of Household income from VP	Reduced transportation costs (phone as substitute)	% of airtime minutes sold per phone per day/week/month	% of airtime minutes sold per phone per day/week/month
Incremental sales increase in main business due to VP business	Employment impacts (VPO hiring others in community)	% of VPOs sustainable/profitable	# of customers in new markets reached
Poverty level differences		% of VPOs who repaid loan, default rate on VP loans	
Less income volatility; daily cash flow covers expenses		MFI VP product profit margin (cost of VP support, staff resources); cost savings	MTN VP product profit
Productivity; ability to earn income from multiple businesses		MFI VP business net income	MTN VP business unit net income & profitability (EBITDA)

Socio-Cultural Impact	
VPO	**Community**
Decision-making impact and role within household and community (pre & post VP; improved position in borrower group)	Access to public and social services (police/crime, hospital, emergency)
Kinship connection and closeness (across towns, distances, bridges geographic dispersion); bigger social network	Kinship connection and closeness (across towns, distances, bridges geographic dispersion)
Support structure for VPO in community (borrower group, family & friends)	Social interactions (seek out VPO, may not have known/interacted before)
Perception of VPO in community (social status, distinction, valued service, VPO as role model for community & women, VPO status as an incentive for education)	Perception of VPO in community (social status, distinction, valued service, VPO as role model for community & women, VPO status as an incentive for education)
Social equilibrium (VPO household treated better & interacted with more by well-off households, technology access creates social advantage, etc.)	Access to news and cultural information; Participate in larger community (radio w/phone links people politically)

VILLAGE PHONE MODEL VARIANTS AND EXTENSIONS

This manual describes a particular Village Phone model and implementation. It is hoped that the dialogue herein provides insight into the decisions made at various points along the way and also insight into the options considered. Following these alternate decisions paths can lead to a very different Village Phone model and implementation. This will of course be driven largely by the unique environment and partners.

Outside the obvious decisions paths, there are different models which perhaps are not highlighted. For example, the Village Phone Company could deploy physical network infrastructure and provide an extension to the Telecom Operators network infrastructure. Deployment would be to areas where the entrenched Operator would be unprepared to deploy equipment – such a partnership could satisfy regulatory or licensing requirements for the Telecom Operator. Licensing would have to be a consideration in such a model. Village Phone Company could deploy solar powered micro-cells with a link to core network back-haul by low cost microwave links. Revenue could be through roaming agreements with the Telecom Operator.

MICROFINANCE AS A CHANNEL TO MARKET

The success of this program can be measured by the thousands of new micro enterprises created, and also by the millions of people who benefit from having affordable communications and information services in their village. One further success which bears elaboration is the establishment of the microfinance sector as a powerful ally to commercial interests – a recognition that millions of additional 'customers' can be reached by a channel to market infrastructure that exists, is strong, transacting financially, and is supported by social networks unheard of in traditional markets. Further, synergies exist that can be crafted into mutually beneficial business relationships where doing well financially also means being instrumental in catalyzing significant positive social change.

Village Phone demonstrates that the microfinance sector acting as a channel to market works. It also alludes to a myriad of possible permutations for delivering valuable goods and services to the rural poor who are consumers but are not able to participate in the marketplace because these products remain in urban centers.

CREATING INFRASTRUCTURE

Village Phone has created a communications infrastructure in the rural communities. This is more than the technical infrastructure – it is the channel to market, the distribution, sales, marketing and store-front infrastructure that enables people to make use of the technical infrastructure in a way that makes it personal for them. Upon such an infrastructure can be built such public and commercial services as can be imagined:

> *Village Phones Transfer Money*
> *In Uganda, one UWFT client is using his Village Phone as a money transfer tool through text messaging. In the rural county of Buhweju in Bushenyi district, where transport from the villages to the town centers is limited, the Village Phone has facilitated a number of transactions. The Operator is based at a rural secondary school and has become the major means through which school fees and for the pupils is paid. The parents buy airtime from the U-Trust branch and send the access number as a message to the operator who then pays the airtime cash equivalent to the school or gives the money to the pupils.*

- Village Phone Operators can become early warning network for disaster prevention and mitigation.
- Village Phone Operators can gather, monitor and report community heath metrics with software applications built into the phone.
- Governments can use SMS to communicate widely through Village Phone Operators.
- Village Phone Operators can evolve into Village Information Providers.
- Commercial interests could partner with Village Phone to offer free SMS messages funded. through appended advertising to a sent or received SMS message
- Banks and microfinance organizations could offer transaction services through secure SMS sent from a Village Phone.

- Airtime could become a de-facto currency and goods and services could be transferred between virtual accounts paving the way for a distributed payment system.

We encourage others to take advantage of the infrastructure created by Village Phone and also to explore additional innovative partnerships with the microfinance sector to bring much needed opportunities and products to a new and eager market.

Building upon the Village Phone infrastructure, future technology innovations have a great platform from which to launch and provide additional features, products and services into these deep rural locations where Village Phone Operators serve their communities. Imagine the potential services expansion enabled by 3G communications technologies or long-range wireless Internet connectivity.

CASE STUDY – VILLAGE PHONE IN BANGLADESH

Organizations involved

There are four parties that work together in Bangladesh to bring telecommunications service to rural villagers:

- *GrameenPhone (GP):* GrameenPhone is a for-profit telecommunications company in Bangladesh. They are responsible for establishing and maintaining the physical communications infrastructure used in the Village Phone program. GrameenPhone liaisons with Grameen Telecom to provide services to the Village Phone Operators at discounted rates. GrameenPhone is also responsible for complying with government regulations.
- *Grameen Telecom (GT):* Grameen Telecom is a for-profit organization with the mission of providing telecommunication services to the rural, and radically underserved, areas of Bangladesh. Grameen Telecom is responsible for coordinating the Village Phone Program, working with GrameenPhone and Grameen Bank. Grameen Telecom supplies equipment to the Village Phone Operators and also provides support services to the Village Phone Operators through its service centers and the call center. Grameen Telecom acts as the liaison between GrameenPhone and Grameen Bank for transfer of bills and payments.
- *Grameen Bank (GB):* Grameen Bank is a microfinance organization in Bangladesh that provides credit to the poorest of the poor. Grameen Bank provides loans to the Village Phone Operators to buy the hardware equipment from Grameen Telecom. Also, Grameen Bank serves as the first level of contact between the Village Phone Operators and Grameen Telecom for bill repayments and support services.
- *Village Phone Operator:* The Village Phone Operator is the communications service provider for the community. The Village Phone Operator provides the service to the end user, collects payments, and remits the same to

Grameen Bank (who forwards them on to Grameen Telecom and then GrameenPhone).

Results

At the end of 2004, over 87,500 Village Phone businesses had been established throughout rural Bangladesh – a phenomenal accomplishment. These phones are used on average for 58 minutes per day for both incoming and outgoing calls.

Number of Village Phone Operators in Bangladesh 1997-2004

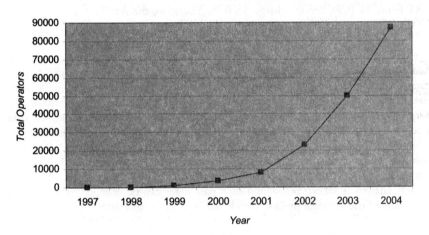

Success for GrameenPhone

The Village Phone program has been quite successful for GrameenPhone. In March 2001, the average revenue per phone was $93 per month, twice as much as GrameenPhone's average urban customer.[16] By 2003, Village Phones accounted for approximately 16% of total airtime sold by GrameenPhone, although only 4% of the company's total customer base.[17]

Village Phone Operator Sustainability

Village Phone Operators across Bangladesh have established very profitable businesses and a clear path out of poverty. Operators in Bangladesh earn an average net income of $58 per month from their Village Phone businesses. The impact of middlemen has been drastically reduced in rural market transactions and the social status of women has increased as a result of their Village Phone businesses.

---

[16] World Resources Institute Digital Dividend. *What Works: Grameen Telecom's Village Phones.* http://www.digitaldividend.org/case/case_grameen.htm
[17] Grameen Bank website: http://www.grameen-info.org/bank/GBGlance.htm

GrameenPhone describes the financial mechanism for the Village Phone operators as follows:

"GrameenPhone charges are Taka 2.00 per minute for local calls at peak hour (compared to Taka 4.00 for urban subscribers). For NWD and ISD calls, GP charges BTTB rate plus VP air time charges. 15% Value Added Tax (VAT) is added to total call charges. To compensate the administrative costs incurred by GTC and GB, 15% service charge are added to the total GP bill. VP Operators are supplied with a price list that includes all kinds of charges and a margin of profit for themselves. For example, for a local mobile call, retail rate is Tk 5, out of which GP cost is Tk 2.00, VAT being Tk 0.30, Service charge Tk 0.30. Therefore the rest Tk 2.40 is the profit for the VP Operator." [18]

The Village Phone businesses are started with a loan from Grameen Bank which is paid back in weekly payments over a two year period. An important role that the microfinance institutions plays is to help the Village Phone Operators understand how to monitor the health of their business and attain sustainability. Each Village Phone Operator should know how many minutes per day their phone needs to be used for their business to break even (including meeting the microfinance institution's financial obligations). This number will change based on the size of the loan and payment details. The business becomes unsustainable when the operator can no longer meet financial obligations to the microfinance institution. The basis for this analysis is shown below and each parameter can be changed to address the particulars of the financial product developed by your organization.

---

[18] Grameen Telecom website: http://www.grameen-info.org/grameen/gtelecom/

VPO Revenue		
Average VPO margin per minute	$	0.043
Average minutes per day		58
Total daily revenue	$	2.49
Total weekly revenue	$	17.46

VPO Loan		
Equipment pricing	$	250.00
Loan Term		92
Loan Periodicity		1
Interest Rate		21%
Weekly loan obligiation	$	3.26
Cumpulsory savings*	$	2.50
Total weekly payment	$	5.76

Analysis - Daily		
VPO Income	$	2.49
VPO loan obligations	$	0.82
Surplus after loan repayment	$	1.67

# of min/day for breakeven during loan	
	19.12

*Note: Grameen Bank has a compulsory savings program which requires their clients to place 1% of their loan principal into savings every week.

Success for Grameen Bank

The Village Phone product has proven to be very successful for Grameen Bank. Over 95% of the Village Phone Operators repay their loans, providing a steady source of income for the bank.[19]

Market specific success keys

Bangladesh is ideally suited for a Village Phone program. It has an extremely high population density (958 per sq. km in 2003 – the country has a population of over 140 million)[20] and a teledensity of only 0.79 telephone subscribers per 100 inhabitants.[21] This results in a very high demand for telecommunications.

The topography of Bangladesh is extremely flat. As a result, there are few natural impediments to extending the range of GrameenPhone's mobile telecommunications infrastructure with the use of Yagi antennas.

The Village Phone program in Bangladesh was able to start in large part due to the "common DNA" that existed across the three Grameen organizations involved in launching the program. Grameen Bank, GrameenPhone, and Grameen Telecom were all able to leverage the strength of the Grameen name and their organizational linkages to forge Village Phone.

---

[19] Mohammed Masud Isa , Managing Director and Chief Executive Officer , Grameen Telecom: http://www.dse.de/ef/digital/isa-e.htm
[20] CIA world factbook, July 2003
[21] World Telecommunication Development Report 2003, International Telecommunication Union

Many looked to Bangladesh and said that the only reason Village Phones are successful is because of these unique market conditions. The Village Phone Uganda initiative has demonstrated that success is not limited to Bangladesh.

CASE STUDY – VILLAGE PHONE IN UGANDA

Six parties that came together in Uganda to bring telecommunications service to rural villagers:

- *MTN Uganda (MTNU)* – *"Telecommunications partner"*. MTN Uganda is a subsidiary of the MTN Group, a listed South African multi-national company with operations in eight African countries. MTNU is Uganda's largest telecommunications provider with over 400,000[22] subscribers.
- *MTN publiCom (MTNP)* - *"Colleague in Public Access and Fixed Wireless Devices"*. MTN publiCom is an associated company of MTN Uganda operating public payphones throughout Uganda. MTNP currently has over 2000 fixed wireless devices (phone booths or fixed call boxes) deployed across Uganda with the majority being deployed in urban centers. MTNP was created to meet MTN Uganda's obligation to the Ugandan government to ensure public access communication.
- *MTN villagePhone* – *"The Village Phone Company"*. To manage the day-to-day operations of the Village Phone program, a new company was established in Uganda called MTN villagePhone. MTN villagePhone is a 50-50 partnership between MTN-Uganda and Grameen Foundation USA, with both parties as equal shareholders and investors. MTN villagePhone has four staff members and a five member board of directors (two from MTN-Uganda, two from Grameen Foundation USA, and one independent).
- *Microfinance Institutions (MFIs)* - *"The Market Channel"*. Microfinance institutions are significant to Uganda's poverty alleviation. They responded to communities' needs with innovative offerings including individual and group credit schemes and 'micro'-insurance on health and life. They have pursued ad-hoc initiatives to bring information and communication technologies to the rural communities. As of 2005, seven microfinance institutions are in partnership with MTN villagePhone:
  - UWFT (an affiliate of Women's World Banking): >70,000 members
  - FOCCAS (an affiliate of Freedom from Hunger): >20,000 members
  - FINCA (an affiliate of FINCA International): >40,000 members
  - UMU (ACCION International): >50,000 members
  - MedNet (an affiliate of World Vision): >12,000 members
  - Feed the Children: > 14,000 members
  - Hofokam: > 15,000 members
- *Village Phone Operators* – *"The Retailer"*. As the business operators and core beneficiaries, Village Phone Operators are the primary stakeholders. Village

---

[22] As of October 2003

Phone Operators are all existing microfinance institution clients and are selected to be the communications service provider for their community based on their loan repayment record, position in the community, location and business capabilities.

- *Grameen Technology Center/Grameen Foundation USA – "The Catalyst"*. The Grameen Technology Center is an initiative of Grameen Foundation USA, a non-profit organization (NGO) based in the United States which empowers the world's poorest people to lift themselves out of poverty with dignity through access to financial services and to information. Grameen approached MTN to propose the Village Phone Uganda project and has transferred knowledge and experience from the Grameen Village Phone program in Bangladesh.

Market specific success keys

A number of strategic decisions were made when replicating Village Phone in Uganda that have proven to be instrumental to the program's success:

Unlike Bangladesh where there is one microfinance institution partner (Grameen Bank), there are seven different microfinance partners in Uganda. Each one was allowed to tailor their own loan product for their customers, offering different loan durations and interest rates.

An optional incentive scheme for microfinance institution loan officers was introduced allowing them to share in the profits of the program. This also served as an excellent incentive to encourage the deployment of new village phones.

MTN proved to be an excellent partner for Grameen Foundation USA in Uganda. Their commitment as a partner and willingness to assist in marketing, infrastructure, and logistical support has made a huge impact in the success of the program

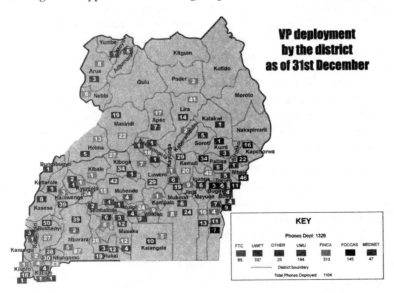

Village Phone deployments shown by MFI Partner as of December 31, 2004

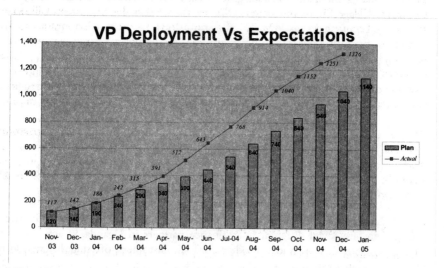

Village Phone actual deployments in Uganda vs. expected deployments

CLOSING THOUGHTS

This manual is intended to share the Village Phone model and so catalyze a worldwide Village Phone movement. We are certain that this movement will occur and will take many forms. Many of these efforts to bring telecommunications services to the un-served communities living in the developing world may not even remotely resemble the forms and practice as described in this manual. We have documented what is, we hope, best practice for the environment of Uganda and trust that you can extract the essence as it applies to your particular set of circumstances and environment and replicate the principles and evolve the specific practices to suit.

Of all the particular processes, procedures, systems and infrastructure necessary to launch and succeed in an initiative such as Village Phone, we assert strongly that there is nothing more important that the relationships between the partners – a shared vision, commitment, persistence, hard work, trust and honesty. These above all will lead to success.

IN THE PUBLIC DOMAIN

The information presented herein is shared in the spirit of international cooperation and it is intended that this document remain in the public domain. We ask that all users of this manual similarly share any modifications, variants, and/or lessons learned from experience so that new information can be incorporated into the broader learning of the global Village Phone movement.

Grameen Foundation USA will continue to act as a clearinghouse for Village Phone replication information and promote the Village Phone movement. We expect to publish new versions of this manual in the future as the movement evolves.

APPENDIX A: VILLAGE PHONE RESOURCES AND PUBLICATIONS

TeleCommons Development Group Case Study (CIDA)
http://www.telecommons.com/villagephone/contents.html

World Resources Institute Digital Dividend – What Works: Grameen Telecom's Village Phones
http://www.digitaldividend.org/pdf/grameen.pdf

World Bank Case Study:
http://poverty.worldbank.org/files/14648_Grameen-web.pdf

Video
http://www.cnn.com/SPECIALS/2000/virtualvillages/story/bangladesh/
http://www.gfusa.org/docs/technology_center/GFUSA-VillagePhone2Min-web.wmv

GrameenPhone Overview
The Village Phone program is GrameenPhone's unique method of bringing connectivity to the rural areas of Bangladesh.
http://www.grameenphone.com/modules.php?name=Content&pa=showpage&pid=3

International Labour Organization
This paper will reflect on market development outcomes due to the ICT services provided by Grameen Telecom. We will look at the reality of Bangladeshi village economy as the context for which this market intervention has been designed and implemented
http://www.ilo.org/public/english/employment/ent/papers/grameen.htm

UNDP/Markle Foundation
Final report of the Digital Opportunity Initiative (2001)
http://www.opt-init.org/framework/pages/appendix2Case2.html

WRI Digital Dividends
Rural Connectivity: Grameen Telecom's Village Phones
http://www.digitaldividend.org/pdf/grameen.pdf

Information Impacts
By any measure, Grameen Bank is a success story. What worked? (December 1999)
http://www.cisp.org/imp/december_99/12_99camp.htm

World Association for Christian Communication
Isn't it ridiculous to suggest that mobile phones can improve the lives of rural poor people? Sean Hawkey finds out in Bangladesh.
http://www.wacc.org.uk/publications/action/241/grameen_telecom.html

IPAN
'GrameenPhone Sewa' by Escotel connects over 450 villages in UP (West) and Haryana
New Delhi, January 09, 2001
http://www.ipan.com/PRESS/2001jan/0901esc.htm

Wall Street Journal
A Village in Bangladesh By MIRIAM JORDAN - June 25, 1999
http://www.idsusa.org/MicroCredit/CellPhone.htm

The Communication Initiative
GRAMEEN VILLAGE PHONE
http://www.comminit.com/11-342-case_studies/sld-643.html

Grameen Dialogue (Newsletter Published by the Grameen Trust)
New Technology for Poverty Alleviation: Rural Phones Service Is Profitable In Poor Countries
http://asp.grameen.com/dialogue/dialogue47/specialfeature.html

Asian Development Bank
Phone Loan / Wiring Bangladesh-Without Wires - GrameenPhone: good business can mean good development
http://www.adb.org/Documents/Periodicals/ADB_Review/2001/vol33_2/wired.asp

CNN
Virtual Villages: Technology and the Developing World – Bangladesh
http://www.cnn.com/SPECIALS/2000/virtualvillages/story/bangladesh/

BBC
Mobile money spinner for women.
http://news.bbc.co.uk/2/hi/technology/2254231.stm

UNESCO
A micro-credit program set up by Grameen Bank enables rural villagers to acquire cell phones. For many, it means a break with poverty and isolation
http://www.unesco.org/courier/2000_07/uk/connex2.htm#top

International Journal of Economic Development
An assessment of microfinance programs in Uganda
http://www.spaef.com/IJED_PUB/v1n1_barnes.PDF

MTN villagePhone Documentary (13 Minutes)
http://www.gfusa.org/docs/technology_center/GFUSA-VillagePhone2Min-web.wmv

MTN villagePhone Video Summary (1 Minute)
Created by Tech Museum Awards Committee
http://www.gfusa.org/docs/technology_center/GFUSA-VillagePhoneTechAwards.mov

APPENDIX B: TEMPLATE MOU

TERMS OF AGREEMENT
AN MOU
between
Village Phone Company
and
MFI

This terms agreement outlines the agreement made between *MFI* and *Village Phone Company*. This terms agreement is not designed to be a legal document but is intended to specify the roles and responsibilities of each party to this agreement in relation to the shared goal of bringing mobile phone services to MFI members in rural *Country*. Once mutually ratified, this terms agreement can be formalized in a legal form.

Village Phone Company agrees to:

1. Make available for purchase "Village Phone Kits" for purchase at the *Distribution Center*. These kits will include mobile phone, tariff sheet, signage and other marketing collateral, and documentation. Options for an external antenna and recharging solution will also be available.
2. Work with *MFI* to provide marketing for the Village Phone Program. This may include print ad and radio media.
3. Negotiate favorable rates for Village Phone Operators for communication services provided by *Telecom Operator*.
4. Facilitate Distribution Agreement between *MFI* and *Telecom Operator* for sale of airtime cards to Village Phone Operators
5. Assist in evaluating network coverage in rural villages where *MFI* operates
6. Train *MFI* staff in use and support of mobile phones
7. Train a core staff at *MFI* to enable them to train Village Phone Operators in the operational aspects of the business
8. Provide a detailed Village Phone Manual to *MFI* and Village Phone Operators
9. Provide monthly reports to *MFI*
10. Advise *MFI* of changes in network coverage
11. Coordinate media efforts
12. Facilitate general problem solving
13. Include *MFI* in marketing efforts where possible and appropriate
14. Make available via telephone customer support during normal business hours
15. Enter into a reciprocal non-disclosure agreement with *MFI*

MFI agrees to:

1. Develop a plan to deploy Village Phones within the rural MFI network in *Country*. Such a plan will indicate deployment goals and districts for Village Phone activities. As an introduction to the partnership, this plan could include a pilot initiative.
2. Execute the deployment plan utilizing the best efforts of *MFI* to reach the goals
3. Identify individuals to participate as "Village Phone Operators" in the Village Phone program
4. Work through the existing lending processes and structures to ensure community support for the prospective Village Phone Operators business launch
5. Work with the prospective Village Phone Operator to submit a proposal to Village Phone for this business (pro-forma will be provided), including specific location for this prospective business
6. Provide credit finance to Village Phone Operators
7. Purchase and deliver "Village Phone Kits", including hardware equipment to Village Phone Operators
8. Train Village Phone Operators in the use of the mobile phone and operation of the Village Phone business. Such training should be in groups of Village Phone Operators to ensure efficient use of *MFI* resources in this training. *Village Phone Company* will train MFI staff to enable this to occur.
9. Enter into a Distribution relationship with Telecom Operator in order to on-sell prepaid phone cards exclusively to Village Phone Operators. *MFI* will be entitled to x% of each card sold.
10. Through the usual periodic meetings, make best efforts to ensure that the Village Phone Operators always have sufficient airtime for resale
11. Record deployment details for each Village Phone Operator (name, location, number, etc)
12. Record baseline information regarding the Village Phone Operator to facilitate the ongoing evaluation of the Village Phone Program and its impact on individuals and communities. Such information should include, at a minimum, income, poverty level, demographic details, etc..
13. Work with *Village Phone Company* to solve service problems (as necessary)
14. Participate in Strategic Planning with *Village Phone Company* to define the scope of future services
15. Assist the Village Phone Operators to the extent possible as they work to resolve problems when their phone is inoperable
16. Through the usual periodic Village Group meetings, make best efforts to ensure and monitor that phones and SIM cards are only used by Village Phone Operators in their designated locations and for the purpose of providing a community communications resource
17. Report repayment rates and other metrics to *Village Phone Company* for use in analyzing program success
18. Enter into a reciprocal non-disclosure agreement

_____   _____

Name: Name:
For: *Village Phone Company*   For: *MFI*

Dated this ………. Day of ……………..…., *200X*

APPENDIX C: MICROFINANCE MANUAL FOR VILLAGE PHONE

Note: This is available as a separate document if needed.

VILLAGE PHONE

PROGRAM MANUAL FOR MICROFINANCE INSTITUTIONS

Version: Template V1.0

January 2005

1.0 WELCOME

Congratulations on becoming a key partner in the Village Phone business in *Country*. Your participation as a microfinance institution is critical to the success of the program. In partnership with *Village Phone Company*, you will be instrumental in providing much needed affordable communications services to your members across your areas of operation. Your participation will generate an additional income stream for your organization and at the same time provide a profitable business opportunity for your members, who will become Village Phone Operators (Village Phone Operators) within their rural communities.

2.0 BACKGROUND

2.1 Grameen's Village Phone Program- Success in Poverty Reduction

One of the greatest success stories in international development has been Grameen's Village Phone Program in Bangladesh. In rural villages where no telecommunications service has previously existed, cellular phones are provided to very poor women who use the phone to operate a business providing communications services to her community. At the close of 2000, there were 3273 village phones deployed. By early 2005, there were over 87,000 Village Phones deployed in poor rural villages of Bangladesh. Airtime usage per phone has also increased and is on average more than five times that of an urban phone.

The most obvious benefit of the Village Phone program is the economic impact that telecommunications access brings to the entire village / parish. There is clear evidence of this impact from Bangladesh, including higher prices paid to Village Phone users for their agricultural produce or manufactured goods and better exchange rates when repatriating funds. For the cost of a phone call, a family is able to save the expense of sending a productive member to deliver or retrieve information by traveling great distances in person.

> *"Farmers from the villages use the phones to call the city markets to find out prices for their produce. Previously they were a little bit short-changed by their middlemen. The middlemen would say a lower price than what the actual market price was. So now they can call the market themselves to find out what the actual price of eggs or whatever their produce is. An independent study found that half the people who use the phones regularly, traders in rice or bananas for example, make more money from their business and they save 10 hours in travel time."*

> *"If the Grameen Telecom experience is a reliable guide, then providing phone service yields powerful social and economic benefits in rural communities....Empowering poor communities by providing a wide range of digitally enabled self-help tools – via the private sector – could become a crucial part of an effective rural development strategy ... Business is a proven method of solving their [the poor] problems in a sustainable way."*

In a Canadian International Development Agency (CIDA) commissioned study, it was concluded that the Grameen Village Phone program yields "significant positive social and economic impact, including relatively large consumer surplus and immeasurable quality of life benefits". The study concluded that the consumer surplus for a single phone call ranges from 2.64% to 9.8% of mean monthly household income. The cost of a trip to the city ranges from two to eight times the cost of a single phone call, meaning that the real savings for poor rural people is between $2.70 and $10.00 for individual calls. The income that Village Phone Operators derive from the Village Phone is about 24% of the household income on average – in some cases it was as high as 40% of the household income.

Most importantly, Village Phone Operators become socially and economically empowered. Some creative and entrepreneurial users of the technology identify new business opportunities, including the resale of information to others in their communities. The technology also serves to link regional entrepreneurs with each other and their clients, bringing more business to small enterprises. Grameen's experience in Bangladesh has shown that information technology has enormous potential for increasing local economic activity and business opportunities.

Because the phone operators are typically female and the phones are in their places of business, women who might otherwise have very limited access to a phone, feel comfortable using one. Furthermore, as these phones become so important for the whole village, the status of women in the communities where they work is enhanced.

> *"Phones have helped elevate the status of the female phone operators in the village. Surveys have found that the Village Phone Operators become socially empowered as they earn an income, gaining participation in family decisions in which, in rural Bangladeshi society, women usually have no say."*

> *"... [Grameen Village Phone] has had considerable development benefits. It has reduced the cost of communications relative to other services such as transportation....the program has enabled the village pay phone entrepreneurs, poor by most standards but among the better-off in their villages, to turn a profit."*

Having established the infrastructure and institutional framework for such a venture, the poor become the drivers of their own destiny and the experts in the utilization of this technology to their own best advantages – telecommunications is a powerful catalyst and facilitator of such grassroots, self directed development :

> *"Isolation and lack of information [communications] are very serious obstacles to poverty eradication"*

> *"People lack many things: jobs, shelter, food, health care and drinkable water. Today, being cut off from basic telecommunications services is a hardship almost as acute as these other deprivations, and may indeed reduce the chances of finding remedies to them."*

2.2. Replicating the Grameen Model

The success of the program in Bangladesh and Uganda prompted *Your Organization* to consider possible countries where the model could be replicated.

Include your research on poverty, teledensity, - Why is Village Phone a fit for this country?

> *[For example: Working in Uganda in the development sector, you will obviously be aware that Uganda is a poverty-stricken nation, ranking 150 in the UNDP Human Development Index (2000). The waiting list for access to a fixed line telephone is 3.6 years. The teledensity is 1.72 (1.72 telephones- fixed and wireless- for every 1000 people). These telephones are concentrated primarily in urban areas making rural access to telecommunications services difficult and costly. This is despite the fact that Uganda has a population of 23,985,712, with only 14% of the population living in urban centers.]*

It was with this premise, that *Your Organization* and *Telecom Operator* launched an initiative to replicate the success of the Village Phone program in *Country*. The initiative has the following goals:

1. To provide the rural communities of *Country* with valuable communications services to enable them to break the cycle of poverty
2. Other goals as determined

3.0 STRUCTURE OF THE PROGRAM

3.1 Roles and Responsibilities

There are five parties that are needed to make this program a success. The following graphic illustrates their roles and responsibilities: *(Customize for your environment)*

Telecom Operator
- Provide and validate communications coverage to needed rural areas
- Source, stock and on-sell all equipment for *Village Phone Company*
- Sell prepaid airtime cards to MFIs
- Usage data to *Village Phone Company*
- Government licensing & regulation compliance
- Customer Care centre for VPOs
- Strategic planning with partners
- Brand marketing
- Provision of financial services to *Village Phone Company*
- Provide access to office space & facilities

Initial Catalyst/Champion
- Manage initial MFI enrollment and agreements
- Develop Operations Manual
- Develop VPO Manual and MFI Manual
- Strategic planning with partners

Village Phone Company
- Strategic planning, program monitoring & evaluation
- Relationship management with MFI partners
- Development of partner relationships for program expansion
- General problem solving
- Financial management
- Drive and plan network expansion
- Support of VPOs and MFIs
- Coordinate media and PR with *Telecom Operator*
- Training of MFI staff
- Knowledge consolidation and dissemination
- Usage reporting to MFIs
- Marketing

Microfinance Institution (MFI)
- Process VPO selection, applications & appointments
- Credit finance to VPO for purchase of phone & starter kits
- Conduit for equipment to VPOs
- Channel to market
- Conduit for airtime cards to VPOs
- Strategic planning with partners
- Customer support and problem solving for VPO
- Monitor appropriate use of phones and airtime
- Monitoring, evaluation and reporting of VPO performance

Village Phone Operator (VPO)
- Marketing of Village Phone business
- User billing and payment collection
- Airtime purchasing through MFI
- Providing communications service to the community using VP approved tariffs
- A communications knowledge resource to the community
- Equipment maintenance

3.2 Distribution Agreement with Telecom Operator

[It should be determined which is the most appropriate process for utilizing the MFI as a channel to market. These paragraphs below build from the Uganda model and are not necessarily the best way for your particular environment]

The agreement with *Village Phone Company* contains more specific information about the roles and responsibilities of Village Phone and *microfinance organization.*

As a distributor of *Telecom Operator* prepaid phone cards, *microfinance organization* will earn *[To Be Negotiated]* % (see section 5.3 in this document for information on the microfinance institution Incentive Program) on all airtime sold through your network of Village Phone Operators. *Microfinance organization* will enter into a Distribution agreement with *Telecom Operator.* This agreement will place strict guidelines on the scope of your sales activities of prepaid airtime cards. It is in *microfinance organization's* interest to insist that your network of Village Phone Operators only purchase their additional airtime cards from you. Later in this manual there is a detailed analysis of your revenue potential.

3.3 Geographic Distribution

The goal of *Village Phone Company* is to provide communications access to as many poor rural people as possible utilizing the Village Phone shared access model. As such, the partnership model has been designed to ensure that there are open avenues to access these services for all microfinance institution members, regardless of their particular affiliation. Therefore, there can be no dedicated 'franchise areas' where a particular microfinance institution has sole rights to deploy phones. Rather, it is possible that within a particular district there will be more than one microfinance institution deploying phones amongst their membership. A district may contain many microfinance institution partners and Village Phone Operators.

[Optional per your chosen operational model] One key element of success of the Village Phone model is the business viability of each Village Phone Operator. One critical role that *microfinance organization* plays as partner in this model is to work with prospective Village Phone Operators to evaluate the location of their business with respect to competition. Are other Village Phone Operators located near, are there fixed line options (fixed line is often much cheaper than wireless and so the competitive position for a prospective Village Phone Operator will be weak)? *Village Phone Company* will not guarantee zones of 'non-competition' and the success of the Village Phone business to be created will be largely contingent upon appropriate location.

[Optional per your particular chosen methodology] Village Phone is not designed to meet the needs of the urban or peri-urban communities. The goal of the program is to provide communications services where no such viable, affordable, accessible alternatives exist – this is in the rural areas of *Country* where the average villager travels over 2 kilometers to make a call and can pay up to three times the usual retail tariff per minute. Village Phones should not be deployed in urban or peri-urban

areas and the tariff rates are not designed to compete with the myriad of operators on the streets and booths of every urban centre across *Country*. They have been designed to provide affordable communications services to all rural people.

4.0 PLANNING FOR SUCCESS

4.1 Microfinance Institution Financing

Village Phone Company has partnered with *microfinance organization* as a microfinance institution to draw upon the synergy in this relationship. *Village Phone Company* provides the infrastructure, managerial and institutional support to make this program work. You as the microfinance institution provide access to your network of members and your financial services expertise. *Village Phone Company* is not equipped to assist in the sourcing of funds to capitalize your on-lending portfolio for your participation in the program; however, we have been able to broker relationships with institutions such as *[Local Funders, Banks, Government Programs, etc… which operate in Country]* Involvement in the contractual arrangements is outside the scope and capabilities of *Village Phone Company*; however, *Village Phone Company* can catalyze and facilitate ongoing discussions between you and the these organizations. If your organization requires an introduction or a letter or referral and confirmation of partnership, then this can be arranged by contacting the Manager, *Village Phone Company*.

4.2 Deployment Planning

Critical to reaching the goal of deploying *[Number of Planned Deployments]* Village Phones over *[Planning period]* is the planning process undertaken by *Village Phone Company* . As a key partner, your input into this process is critical. As you will note in the Agreement between your organization and *Village Phone Company*, your organization will develop a plan outlining your participation in the program. To enable us to collectively execute a plan that will lead us to reach our goal, your documented input is invaluable. A sample plan, which requires completion on an annual basis, is attached.

4.3 Microfinance Institution Single Point Contact and Authority

In order for *Village Phone Company* to respond confidently and in a timely manner to the communications from *microfinance organization*, there must be an agreed protocol for communications. *Microfinance organization* shall select a single point contact person within your organization that will be the channel for all communications. *Village Phone Company* can then be confident when responding to an order or a request that it has been duly authorized within your organization. An MFI Authority Notification form can be seen in *Appendix H*. This shall be completed and submitted to *Village Phone Company* before any correspondence can be acted upon. This authority also ensures a centrally planned deployment of phones within your organization so that you are able to measure progress towards goals and you have a framework for your own monitoring and evaluation activities.

4.4 Confidentiality

Part of your agreement with *Village Phone Company* and *Telecom Operator* is a recognition and commitment to protect the proprietary knowledge of each organization. This agreement is reciprocal and the partner organizations will make best efforts to protect any such knowledge made available. Disclosure of all information produced by or for *Village Phone Company* or *Telecom Operator* must be authorized by *Village Phone Company* prior.

5.0 THE BUSINESS MODEL

5.1 Multiple Partners

There are multiple levels at which this business operates and all must be viable in their own right. There are no subsidies in this business model and each aspect of the overall system operates profitably and sustainability. Consider the model at the various levels:

Project Partner	Business Model	Sustainability Notes and Examples
Telecom Operator	Airtime sales yield profits on prior infrastructure investments	*Telecom Operator* is a corporate entity who wishes to reach a greater customer base in poor rural areas and who recognizes that they can do so profitably using a shared access model and utilizing channel to market and financing infrastructure of microfinance networks.
The Microfinance Institution	The microfinance institution gets a percentage of all airtime used by their network of Village Phone Operators. Additionally, the microfinance institution reaps the benefit of the financing agreement with the Village Phone Operator in terms of interest income.	Revenues to the microfinance partner are based on airtime usage. The marginal cost of delivery is small as they utilize their existing infrastructure to reach their constituency – the Village Phone Operators and their 'customers'.

continued

Village Phone Company	Revenue for this partner is derived from airtime sales.	Revenues cover the management and administration costs for the business.
Village Phone Operator	Sells phone airtime for outgoing calls. Also generates revenue from non-airtime sources such as message delivery and recharging services.	Entrepreneurial driven business creates innovation in the marketplace.

In Bangladesh and Uganda, the lesson learned is that the model works because everyone is a 'winner'.

- The 'customer': sees an immediate financial return (in terms of opportunity costs) and who gets a personalized 'delivery' service
- The Village Phone Operator: makes a profit on the margin between their cost and sale price for airtime – and is also providing a valuable service to the community.
- *The Telecom Operator*: now reaches customers previously economically inaccessible at a small marginal cost and at a lower margin, but at a significantly greater volume yielding much greater revenue per phone than 'normal' urban subscribers.
- Microfinance Institutions: find value in the social yield but also in the ongoing revenue stream from credit agreements from Village Phone Operators and from the airtime sales which perpetuate themselves with little additional resources or input.
- *Village Phone Company*: covers its costs and generates a surplus in which to extend its mission driven expansion throughout *Country*.

5.2 Village Phone Operator Revenues

It is important for you to help your Village Phone Operators understand how to monitor the health of their business and attain sustainability. Each Village Phone Operator should know how many minutes per day their phone needs to be used for their business to break even (including meeting the microfinance institution financial obligations). This number will change based on the size of the loan and payment details. The business becomes unsustainable when the operator can no longer meet financial obligations to the microfinance institution. The basis for this analysis is shown below and each parameter can be changed to address the particulars of the financial product developed by your organization. Electronic copies of these worksheets can be provided to assist you in your analysis. Please contact the Manager, *Village Phone Company* if you would like to receive electronic copies.

The business model is built on averages – average number of minutes sold by each Village Phone Operator – some will sell hours, some just a few minutes. There are Village Phone Operators in Uganda consistently selling more than 4 hours (240 minutes) per day of airtime. The sustainability model itself represents an average, but this example breakeven analysis below shows that if a Village Phone Operator is selling less than 16 minutes per day, then they are operating at a deficit while they are within in their 26 week loan repayment period. Because we are dealing with averages, there will be Village Phone Operators operating below this utilization, and there will be those who far exceed this average. Our idealistic goal is to have all Village Phone Operators operating profitably when we consider their Village Phone business as stand-alone.

For those Village Phone Operators operating below the breakeven utilization, we should not consider this non-sustainable or a business failure, nor should we consider this Village Phone Business a burden driving the poor entrepreneur further into poverty. We are working with a system which holistically provides for a sustainable livelihood for the Village Phone Operator and their family. Village Phone Operators should be selected by their communities and by your loan officers as upstanding and respected citizens who have proven their entrepreneurial skills and have established a record of success in their micro-entrepreneurial activities, and their ongoing relationship with the microfinance institution is based upon a solid credit record. The basis of success of the Village Phone Operator business must be considered as a part of the whole, 'internally synergistic livelihood' as discussed above in the table outlining the business model. In this context, it is important to note that after the loan is repaid, the Village Phone Operator's gross revenue is money straight to their family revenue.

VILLAGE PHONE OPERATOR BUDGET & SUSTAINABILITY

VPO Daily Revenue	USD
Average VPO margin per minute	$0.10
Billable minutes sold per day	20
Total Daily Revenue	$2.00

ANALYSIS	USD
VPO Daily Income	$2.00
VPO Daily Financial Obligations	$1.64
(Surplus after loan repayment)	$0.36

Example MFI Financing	
Equipment Pricing (Loan principal)	$240.00
Loan Term (weeks)	26
Loan Periodicity (weeks)	2
Interest Rate (Flat, Monthly)	4%
TOTAL DAILY OBLIGATION	$1.64

Breakeven (During Loan)	
VPO Breakeven Minutes / Day	16.35

Revenue Projection (Post-Loan)	
VPO Revenue Projection	$2.00

5.3 Microfinance Institutions Revenues

[How the Telecom Operator has structured the Distribution Channel will determine how the MFI is compensated for their partnership] The revenues expected for your organization are based upon the success of your Village Phone Operator network. The table below provides a tool to enable you to consider the variables involved and the revenue potential.

Indicative Revenue for MFI (USD)					
	Monthly				
		Number of minutes per day			
		15	20	40	60
# of phones	50	$228	$304	$608	$913
	100	$456	$608	$1,217	$1,825
	500	$2,281	$3,042	$6,083	$9,125
	Annual				
		Number of minutes per day			
		15	20	40	60
# of phones	50	$2,738	$4,260	$8,520	$12,780
	100	$5,475	$7,300	$14,600	$21,900
	500	$27,375	$36,500	$73,000	$109,500

** Note : Airtime income only. Loan income is additional
** Note : Assuming 5% commission on retail price of of $0.20/min

MFI Incentive Program

An Incentive Program has been implemented to encourage MFI branch staff to:

- Make new connections (i.e. sell starter packs)
- Sell airtime
- Maintain required stock levels at branch

The financial incentive, which is an additional *[To be negotiated]* percent discount for airtime and starter-pack sales, is the foundation of the incentive program. *Village Phone Company* and the MFI will agree on and document a customized incentive program that takes account of the unique branch structure and other circumstances pertaining to each MFI. Additional information can be found in the *MFI Incentive Document*, which outlines the intent and sample methodologies for discount allocation and the obligations of *Village Phone Company* and the MFI. To obtain a copy of this document, please contact the Manager, *Village Phone Company* *[This is a document which you will have to create once you establish to policy vis-à-vis incentives]*.

5.4 Prepaid Airtime

According to your own management systems, you may decide to develop controls and processes for management and distribution of an inventory of prepaid phone cards. The airtime cards used by the Village Phones are standard product – it is possible for a Village Phone Operator to purchase airtime from, for example, a service station. It is imperative to your business model that you insist along with your own agreements that the Village Phone Operator purchase airtime from your organization. This obligation is addressed in the Village Phone Operator Agreement, a sample of which can be found in the Village Phone Operator Manual. Should you find misappropriation, you may take any action as you deem necessary, even as far as redeploying that phone to another member (with appropriate coordination with *Village Phone Company*) or requesting that the phone be blocked (see *Appendix G*).

The 'magic' happens with *Telecom Operator*'s back office billing systems that recognizes a particular phone by its SIM and knows it is a Village Phone, and then bills the special village phone rate per minute instead of the usual general public rate. By way of example, a standard *$10* *[Localize all currencies in quantum and currency type]* phone card will provide approximately *[Number of minutes]* of outgoing *[call type]* calls, while with that same *$10* airtime card applied to a village phone, the Village Phone Operator will be able to sell approximately *[Number of Minutes]* minutes of airtime and for each of those minutes pocket a profit.

5.5 Your Microfinance Product

The Village Phone program is needed because every poor rural person in *Country* cannot afford their own phone, and the existing infrastructure of fixed public pay phones is insufficient. The shared access model works because it allows an individual to purchase a set of equipment that enables them to become a communications focal point for their area. The enabling funding comes from the microfinance institution. The social networks that allow this funding to be made available for such a purpose also provide a strong basis for building a loyal customer base.

In the previous section, we have outlined some key parameters associated with the business model for the Village Phone Operator. This analysis draws upon usage modeling and factors in margins for the Village Phone Operator. In designing your financial loan product you will need to take these inputs into account.

Providing financial services is your core competency, it is not the intention of *Village Phone Company* to dictate to you on the product or the methodology which you should use or deliver. Below is a short summary of what we have learned from experience:

- Conservative estimates of airtime usage are 15 minutes per day.
- Average weighted Village Phone Operator margin per minute is *[Currency Amount]*
- Village Phone Operator business will have a 'ramp-up' period (also known as "grace period") during which time the business establishes itself and becomes known as a community resource. This period of time varies according to the level of effort of marketing by the Village Phone Operator, the communication throughout the formal peer lending meetings by microfinance institution field officers, and the location of the Village Phone Operator business. No loan repayments should occur during the grace period.
- The equipment itself is the collateral – no deposit should be required

- The value of the business is the SIM card connection, in addition to the phone itself – the special airtime rates are coded into the SIM card and not the phone. *Village Phone Company* always retains ownership of the SIM card connection.
- Grameen Bank in Bangladesh uses a two year loan product, which is often repaid in less than a year. The methodology used is peer lending and loans are proposed, vetted and approved within these usual frameworks.
- MFIs in Uganda offer loan periods of 4-12 months, though we have found a four month loan to be too aggressive a repayment schedule.
- The peer lending framework also provides a basis for loyal customer support of the business of the Village Phone Operator, as they in fact have a financial stake in the success of the business.
- The equipment costs are shown in *Appendix C* (although this is updated monthly). This is the financed amount.
- The equipment should not be marked up at all by the microfinance institution – it should be passed on to the Village Phone Operator at cost.
- The Village Phone Operator is always a member of the microfinance institution and has current lending obligations. If the Village Phone Operator elects to discontinue membership, then their business is forfeited, and the SIM card and *Village Phone Company* marketing materials (sign and business cards) must be returned to the microfinance institution. If the loan remains outstanding, the microfinance institution reclaims the phone and all equipment as collateral.

Aspects of the product you have to consider:

- Loan duration
- Loan principal
- Grace period
- Effective interest rate
- Loan periodicity and repayment schedule
- Lending methodology (Group, individual, other)
- Different loan principal amounts depending upon kit composition and equipment configuration (refer to section 7.2 of this document)

An agreement between your organization and the Village Phone Operator should be made a part of the deployment process. This *Village Phone Operator Agreement* suggests and affirms the responsibilities of the Village Phone Operator vis-à-vis their commitment to operate the business as a community resource.

As a part of *Village Phone Company*'s ongoing program evaluation we request that you submit the detail of your financing vehicle. The template for such submission is found in *Appendix I.*

Additional Finance Products

Village Phone Company has no specific recommendations on the provision of insurance products to Village Phone Operators to cover the equipment. Grameen in Bangladesh offers no such product and has found it unnecessary. The only consideration which may arise is the additional burdening on the Village Phone Operator business model by the additional cost of the insurance product.

Care should be taken in bundling loan insurance (death, disability) with this offering. Because of the ongoing nature of the business relationship and the value and ownership of the SIM card connection, careful thought should be applied.

6.0 SELECTING VILLAGE PHONE OPERATORS

6.1 Selection Criteria

A key element in the success of the program is the performance of the Village Phone Operators. The appropriate selection of these people is important in terms of risk mitigation for the microfinance institution and also in terms of the program's success (e.g., its ability to meet its goals of providing communications to a wide community of Ugandan's rural poor).

If a Village Phone Operator commences a business, uses the phone for personal use only, and does not make the phone available to the community, we have failed. If the Village Phone Operator is not actively marketing their services, the business may not reach sustainability. If the Village Phone Operator is not adequately steeped in the social obligations of being a member of a peer lending community, then there are a myriad of risks for the community and the microfinance institution. This is why Village Phone Operator selection is critical and an microfinance institution's first priority.

Based upon our experience, we suggest you document a set of selection criteria for Village Phone Operators and also define a process for selection. The following can be used as a guideline, and whatever criteria you use, please document and make then known:

- Regular attendance at peer lending meetings
- High status within the group
- Microfinance Institution member for at least 2 years
- 100% repayment history
- Respected as a community member
- Central location for business operations
- Should have an established 'primary' business

The process to identify Village Phone Operators can begin at the community level and should be driven by demand. It could involve an education component where the microfinance institution makes it known that such a business opportunity exists, outlines the selection criteria and opens the discussion for nominations from within the community. A nomination would be approved at the appropriate level within the microfinance institution. Alternatively, the selection process could begin with the microfinance institution suggesting an appropriate person to the peer lending community. Either way, the selection criteria must be made known and the buy-in and support of the peer community must be gained. These are the keys to success.

6.2 Location, Location, Location

The selection criterion demands that the Village Phone Operator business be centrally located. The business must serve and be in the greatest possible community size in order to have enough demand and be sustainable.

A Village Phone business may not exist on its own. It is anticipated the Village Phone business will be adjunct to an existing primary business, such as a store. The Village Phone Operator will offer services from the store front.

The location of the business should generally be fixed. It is not intended that the Village Phone Operator sets up wherever in a random fashion. This is critical to so that community members have a predictable location where they can find the phone. However, it is recognized that some Village Phone Operator's businesses will serve this intended purpose as they travel from daily marketplace to marketplace and serve those people and communities on market day.

Obviously there can be no Village Phone business where there is no mobile phone signal. External antennas for the mobile phones may be used to acquire (i.e., boost) an existing signal in more remote areas. To validate that a location has coverage, it is important to actually place a call with a mobile phone. Just because the phone shows coverage (e.g., one or two bars of signal strength) does not mean that the phone will work in the location. A phone must show at least 2 bars (out of 6) to be effective and reliable and be within a 35 km line of sight from the *Telecom Operator's* tower / base station.

7.0 THE APPLICATION, APPROVAL AND ORDERING PROCESS

7.1 Application for Deployment

Following the Village Phone Operator selection process, the microfinance institution shall work with the prospective Village Phone Operator to complete an Application for Deployment (*Appendix B*). The application contains all the information necessary for *Village Phone Company* to record the deployment. Once the application has been received, *Village Phone Company* will return the authorized form with an equipment pricing quotation by return fax or email. Please note that an authorized application form and pricing quotation is valid for *30 days*. An order placed after this 30 days is void and a new application will need to be submitted and a new quotation generated.

7.2 Equipment

The Village Phone Operator Manual contains detailed information pertaining to the Starter Kit. *[Configuration of the equipment packages will need to be determined and 'packaged' / 'productized']* There are two 'packages' available, Package A contains all items and Package B contains all items except the charging solutions, as some Village Phone Operators may be in areas where electricity supply is reliable and so will not need the solar charger or the optional battery system charger.

The application for deployment form requires you select either Package A or Package B for each Village Phone Operator. If a particular location has reliable electricity, and you believe that the Village Phone Operator can operate their business successfully without being impacted by an inability to charge their phone, then you should recommend the Village Phone Operator purchase Package B.

An antenna and its associated parts are included in the main package as it has been found that it is a useful tool for the vast majority of Village Phone Operators, and further differentiates them in the marketplace. There are areas where you could travel now that would show zero 'bars' – i.e., no signal strength at all. However, with an antenna, a Village Phone Operator could build a viable business at this location. In these marginal areas, *Village Phone Company* will have to work with you to determine the viability of such businesses prior to making an application for deployment.

Each month, *Village Phone Company* sends the microfinance institutions a *Village Phone Company Equipment Order Form* (see *Appendix C*) with the prices for Package A and Package B applicable for that month. All applications submitted in this month are made based on these costs. This allows the microfinance institution to set expectations with prospective Village Phone Operators.

Once the microfinance institution has received an approved application, they complete this order form based on the quotation and prepare an official order for the equipment on their own pro-forma purchase order. A purchase order should state the name of your organization, the registered address, contact phone numbers and the registration number of the organization. The order form and purchase order should be returned to *Village Phone Company* as the official order.

Equipment is to be picked up at *[Distribution Center]* between *[Opening Hours]*, Monday to Friday. It is important that the microfinance institution takes their order form with them so they can cross-check all their equipment. Payment should be made by check (from a nationally recognized bank) *[credit policies to be set and communicated]*. There are significant penalties for bounced checks and a revocation of any further right to pay by check.

7.3 Equipment Warranty and Repair

Ongoing maintenance and repair of Village Phone equipment is the responsibility of the Village Phone Operator, as outlined in the *Village Phone Operator Manual*. The manual also details the warranty information for each product and procedures for repairing handsets and equipment.

Wherever possible, microfinance institutions should ensure the Village Phone Operator maintains responsibility for their equipment. Only in exceptional circumstances should a microfinance institution or Village Phone Operator contact *Village Phone Company* regarding damaged or defected handsets or other equipment. The responsibility of the microfinance institution is to assist the Village Phone Operator by directing them to call *Village Phone Company's* call centre (see section 8.3) or the appropriate repair center.

If the microfinance institution sees trends in equipment failures, these should be reported to the *Village Phone Company* so that corrective action may be taken.

8.0 PHONE DEPLOYMENT AND TRAINING

8.1 MFI Training

Village Phone Company is committed to training nominated staff within your organization in all aspects of the Village Phone program. Such training shall occur prior to any deployments.

Your nominated staff will be fully equipped to train the prospective Village Phone Operators in the operational, business and financial operations of the village phone business. Staff will also be able to guide them in their understanding of the financial package which you offer them to enable their participation in this business.

8.2 Village Phone Operator Training

It is important to spend time training each of your Village Phone Operators in how to operate their business. A sample agenda for a training session can be found in *Appendix D*. The Village Phone Operator manual is essentially a template for this training. Each Village Phone Operator should be given a copy of the *Program Manual for Village Phone Operators* and every section of the manual should be discussed at the time of deployment.

It will not always be possible for the microfinance institution to accompany the Village Phone Operator to their village to set up the equipment. Therefore, it is important that the microfinance institution, during the training session, demonstrates the process for installing an antenna, solar panel and using the charging solutions. In addition, the Village Phone Operator should be shown how to check that all equipment is fully functional, that there is verified signal reception, how to place a test call and how to test receipt of a call.

Following training, the microfinance institution is responsible for the following:

- Signed *Loan Agreement* between microfinance institution and Village Phone Operator
- Signed Village Phone Ag*reement* between microfinance institution and Village Phone Operator
- Completed *Pillage Phone Deployment Record* (see *Appendix E)*, which should be faxed immediately to *Village Phone Company*
- Completed Demographic form (see *Appendix F*), which should be faxed immediately to *Village Phone Company*

8.3 Business Service and Support

Obligations of the Village Phone Operator

The microfinance institution is typically the first point of call for a Village Phone Operator who has run into trouble with their business; however, the *Program Manual for Village Phone Operators* provides an ongoing resource for the Village Phone Operator as a point of reference for managing and marketing their business. The document includes the obligations of the Village Phone Operator as partners in the *Village Phone Company* business. *[Translation of the Program Manual for Village Phone Operators into local languages should be done.]*

In addition to signing a loan agreement with the microfinance institution, the Village Phone Operator is required to sign the Village Phone Operator Agreement which is attached as *Appendix K.* This document is required to be returned immediately to *Village Phone Company.*

Call Center

As outlined in the Village Phone Operator Manual, *Village Phone Company* has a dedicated customer help number (*[Call Center Phone Number]*) and dedicated staff to field calls. When the Village Phone Operator calls *[Call Center Phone Number]* they receive the same privileges as all *Telecom Operator* clients, including access to staff that speak in their preferred language. *[Toll Free?]*

Temporary and Permanent Blocks on Phones

Should a phone be lost or stolen, you should advise the Village Phone Operator to file a police report. The police report should be attached to a 'Request to Block a Phone' (see *Appendix G*) and this should be faxed to *Village Phone Company* who will take the necessary action to block the phone from further use.

If you feel it is necessary to block a phone because of misappropriation, then you should complete the 'Request to Block a Phone' and fax it to *Village Phone Company*. The authorization on the form should be at the appropriate level within the microfinance institution and this person's authority should be on file with *Village Phone Company* (see *Appendix H*).

9.0 MARKETING AND BUSINESS SUPPORT

As part of a broad marketing plan, *Village Phone Company* will market its products and services, both on a regional and national basis. Where appropriate and when a campaign addresses the Village Phone business, *Telecom Operator* or *Village Phone Company* may at its discretion include the microfinance institution in its marketing.

At both a local and international level, your microfinance institution should be able to leverage your involvement in this program to showcase your leading edge innovation in serving the rural poor of *Country*. Presented in an appropriate manner, this could lead to funding opportunities and at the very least, good public relations exposure. Any independent marketing or PR campaign which references *Telecom Operator*, *Village Phone Company* or *[Your Organization]* should be coordinated with *Village Phone Company* .

The success of your involvement in this program is contingent upon success at its most fundamental level – that of the Village Phone Operator. It is the recommendation of *Village Phone Company* that the microfinance institutions engage in marketing support for Village Phone Operators where possible. This could simply be a mention of the business at regular group / center meetings or more extensively, it could mean parallel marketing and PR campaigns which could draw on local print and radio media.

You should also encourage Village Phone Operators to develop their own marketing skills. This may mean suggesting a partnership between the Village Phone Operator and a third party organization or offering training in entrepreneurship and business development. It could mean making an introduction to another organization that is able to extend the service offering of the Village Phone Operator to include adjunct services and thus expanding the strength of their business. Generic Business cards, upon which a Village Phone Operator can write their respective contact details, have been produced for use by the Village Phone Operators to promote their business. Microfinance institutions will receive an allocation of these cards for distribution and ideas for distribution in their community (see *Village Phone Operator Manual*).

10.0 MONITORING, EVALUATION AND REPORTING

The *Village Phone Company* business aims to provide enabling communications infrastructure for the rural poor of *Country* in a sustainable manner. To measure progress towards these objectives, we must gather data and develop a framework for analysis and interpretation.

As a key partner in this program, it is your responsibility to monitor the business success of the Village Phone Operators within your network. *Village Phone Company* will continually monitor weekly call performance data and share the findings with our partner microfinance institutions. Efficient and honest reporting will satisfy both the needs of the donor community and *Village Phone Company* 's need for data as an important input into improving the program.

Sample MFI Deployment Plan

VILLAGE PHONE DEPLOYMENT PLAN

MFI _____

Authorized Officer: _____

Plan Date (month zero): _____

																											DISTRICT						
MONTH	Adjumani	Apac	Arua	Bugiri	Bundibugyo	Bushenyi	Busia	Gulu	Hoima	Iganga	Jinja	Kabale	Kabarole	Kalangala	Kabermaido	Kamuli	Kapchorwa	Kasese	Katakwi	Kibale	Kiboga	Kisoro	Kitgum	Kotido	Kumi	Lira	Luwero	Masaka	Masindi	Mbale	Mbarara	Moroto
6																																
12																																
18																																
24																																
30																																
36																																
42																																
48																																
54																																
60																																

Plan Notes:

SAMPLE APPLICATION FOR VILLAGE PHONE DEPLOYMENT

Microfinance Organization

MFI Name: _____   Date: _____

Zone, Area, or Branch: _____   Order #: _____

Field Officer: _____

Village Phone Operator Details

Village Phone Operator Name: _____

Spouse Name: _____

Business Location

District: _____

County: _____

Sub-County: _____

Parish: _____

Village _____

Latitude/Longitude (GPS) _____

Estimated Distance (km) to nearest
Public Access phone: _____

Signal Strength (Number of Bars) _____ of a possible _____

Electricity Availability _____ hours / day

Peer Lending Center Leader Approval _____

Authorized MFI Officer Approval _____
(name)

Authorized MFI Officer Approval _____
(signature)

**This Application and associated Equipment Pricing Quotes are valid for 30 days
from the date listed above.**

Return a copy of this completed form to *Village Phone Company* via fax: *[Fax Number]*

Village Phone Company use only

Approved:			
Package:	Package A: Complete Set	Package B: No Charging Solution	

SAMPLE EQUIPMENT ORDER FORM

Vilage Phone Company Order Form

Order Date:	14-Nov-03		
MFI:	MFI		
Pick-up Date:	27-Nov-03		

Description	Quantity	Cost (Including VAT)	Total
PACKAGE A: Samsung R220 SIM Pack & Starter Airtime Car Battery & Adapter Cables Antenna & Adapter Cables Marketing Materials	0	*Price*	
PACKAGE B: Samsung R220 SIM Pack & Starter Airtime Antenna & Adapter Cables Marketing Materials	0	*Price*	
TOTAL DUE			**0**

VILLAGE PHONE OPERATOR TRAINING AGENDA

Examples Village Phone Operator Training Outline
At Deployment and Establishment of a NEW Village Phone Business

Introduction

- Welcome and Congratulations
- Why you have been selected to be a Village Phone Operator
- What it means to be a Village Phone Operator (important community resource)
- The obligations of a Village Phone Operator (roles and responsibilities)
- The Village Phone Operator Training Manual

Understanding the Loan

- Loan amount, duration, principal, periodicity, and repayment schedule
- Grace period
- Effective interest rate
- Lending methodology (Group, individual, other)
- Insurance
- Equipment as collateral
- SIM card connection is the property of the Telecom Operator

Equipment

- The Phone (basic operations, care, charging, warranty)
- Recharging the batteries (solar or battery)
- The Antenna (positioning, warranty)

Business Operations

- Financial basis of the Village Phone business
- Tariffs and services
- Margins for Village Phone Operator
- Breakeven (a discussion in concert with the loan product)
- Airtime purchases
- From whom to purchase (only microfinance institution)
- Process for loading airtime onto Village Phone Account (155)
- Monitoring and maintaining Airtime balance
- Record keeping (phone log)

Marketing

- The roadside sign
- Business cards
- Village Phone market niche
- Radio
- Developing a client base

What Happens if.....

- Something happens to the phone or equipment
- Moving
- Selling the business

Operational Tips

- Airtime buffer and bulk purchases
- Using the phone
- Passwords

SAMPLE VILLAGE PHONE DEPLOYMENT RECORD

Village Phone Operator Name: _____

District: _____

Deployment Date: _____

Phone information

IMEI: _____

SIM #: _____

Phone #: _____

Manufacturer/ Model: _____

Car Battery Serial Number: _____

GPS Coordinates: _____

Installation Details

Antenna Installed (Y/N) _____	Signal Strength (# of bars) _____
Solar Panel Installed (Y/N) ____	Battery charging installed (Y/N) _____
Training completed (Y/N) ____	Manuals Provided (Y/N) _____

Financing Information

Village Phone Operator's Other Business: _____

Current Weekly Income: _____

Total Loan Amount _____	Loan Duration (e.g. 104 weeks) _____
Periodic Payment Amount ____	Loan Period (e.g. weekly) _____

Number of customers/day expectation: _____

Signatures

Village Phone Operator's signature: _____

MFI Officer's signature: _____

Return this completed form to *Village Phone Company* at Fax: *[Fax Number]*

SAMPLE VILLAGE PHONE OPERATOR DEMOGRAPHIC FORM

Village Phone Operator: _____

Phone number: _____

MFI _____

Location of Phone (District & Village): _____

Date of Disbursement: _____

1. Are you married? If so what is your spouse's name?

2. How many children do you have?

3. What is your profession?

4. How much did you earn in a week before joining your microfinance institution?

5. How much do you currently earn in a week?

6. What were the amounts of your first loan and your current loan?

7. What were these loans used for?

8. What loan cycle are you currently in?

9. How many clients do you expect to receive each day with your Village Phone?

10. How far do you think your clients will travel to use your Village Phone?

11. How do you plan on marketing your Village Phone service to your community?

12. Are there other people in your Village who offer the same service (competition)? How much do they charge per unit ?

13. How far do people normally travel to use a phone?

    A. Does the client understand the challenges of starting their new small business and the possibility that it could lose money at some stage?

    B. English level assessment of Village Phone Operator:

Return this completed form to *Village Phone Company* at Fax: *[Fax Number]*

SAMPLE REQUEST TO BLOCK/UNBLOCK A PHONE

Village Phone Operator: _____

Microfinance Institution: _____

Date: _____

Authorized Officer: _____

(name)

Phone number to be affected: _____

Action to be taken (circle one only):   Block   Unblock

Responsible Village Phone Operator: _____

Person making this request: _____

Reason for request: _____

_____

_____

_____

_____

Police Report Attached: _____

Signatures

Microfinance Institution Authorized Officer

_____

Village Phone Operator or Registered Operator

_____

Send this completed form to *Village Phone Company* at Fax: *[Fax Number]*

SAMPLE MFI AUTHORITY NOTIFICATION

MFI: _____

Date: _____

MFI Primary Contact
Person_____

Contact Phone:_____

(This person is the person within your organization who has primary responsibility for the Village Phone Program and is the single point contact for communications and correspondence.)

The following people are duly authorized to:

Name	Position	Location	Authorized signature	Authority: Submit an Application	Authority: Request to Block a Phone

Return this completed form to *Village Phone Company* at Fax: *[Fax Number]*

SAMPLE FINANCING PRODUCT DETAILS

MFI _____

Date: _____

Loan Interest Rate: _____

Commission Fee: _____

Other Fees: _____

Loan Period: _____

Loan Periodicity: _____

Grace Period: _____

Effective Interest Rate: _____

Return this completed form to *Village Phone Company* **at Fax:** *[Fax Number]*

This information is to be kept current.
Any changes should be notified to *Village Phone Company.*

All submissions will be in strictest confidence.

SAMPLE CONTACT DETAILS

Village Phone Company

- Contact name
- Address
- Phone
- Fax
- Email
- Hours of Operation

Distribution Center

Village Phone Company Customer Support

Telecom Operator Customer Service (Network)

Emergency Call

Phone Handset Authorized Service Center

Solar Panel Authorized Service Center

Battery Supplier

VILLAGE PHONE OPERATOR AGREEMENT

NOTE TO MFI FIELD STAFF

THIS UNDERTAKING MUST BE COMPLETED AND SIGNED BY THE Village Phone Operator AND ACCEPTED AND SIGNED BY AN AUTHORISED REPRESENTATIVE OF THE MFI PRIOR TO THE ISSUE OF EQUIPMENT AND A STARTER PACK TO THE Village Phone Operator.

THE MFI FIELD OFFICER MUST: -

1) EXPLAIN ITS CONTENTS TO THE PROSPECTIVE Village Phone Operator
2) ENSURE THAT ALL FIELDS ARE ACCURATELY COMPLETED. ANY INCOMPLETE FIELDS WILL RESULT IN THE APPLICATION BEING REJECTED
3) SEND A COPY OF THIS COMPLETED FORM TO Village Phone Company

entered into between

_____

("the MFI")

of

_____
_____
_____
_____

(insert address)

and

FULL NAME ("the Village Phone Operator")	
IDENTITY NUMBER	
PHYSICAL ADDRESS	
POSTAL ADDRESS	
PROPOSED BUSINESS LOCATION	
NEAREST TOWN	

1. INTRODUCTION

The Village Phone Operator's participation in this project is conditional upon compliance with the conditions detailed herein. The Village Phone Operator gives the MFI the undertakings set out below and agrees to the terms set out below.

2. DEFINITIONS

2.1 **"The business"** means the business of operating a phone as explained in the Village Phone Operator manual.

2.2 **"The loan agreement"** means the loan agreement concluded between the Village Phone Operator and the microfinance institution to record the terms of the loan extended to the Village Phone Operator by the microfinance institution to finance the purchase of the phone.

2.3 *"Telecom Operator"* means *[Legal Name of Telecom Operator Name].*

2.4 **"The Telecom Operator network"** means the telephony network operated under license by *Telecom Operator* in *Country.*

2.5 *"Village Phone Company"* means the *[Legal Name of the Village Phone Company Legal].*

2.6 **"Phone"** and **"Equipment"** means a GSM handset and related accessories, which may include a solar panel or 12 volt charger and an external antenna as well as related cabling and connections.

2.7 **"SIM"** means a subscriber identity module included in the starter pack through which a connection is provided to the *Telecom Operator* network.

2.8 **"Starter pack"** means a pre-paid starter pack supplied by *Village Phone Company.*

2.9 **"The Village Phone Operator Manual"** means the manual published and updated by *Village Phone Company*, in its sole discretion and disseminated to the Village Phone Operator by the microfinance institution, which records methods of operation, procedures, contractual terms and other matters relevant to the business.

3. AGREEMENT

3.1 The Village Phone Operator's entitlement to remain connected to the *Telecom Operator* network through the SIM is subject to the Village Phone Operator complying in all respects and at all times with the provisions of the *Village Phone Operator Manual* and this Agreement.

3.2 The microfinance institution retains the right to temporarily or permanently disconnect the SIM from the *Telecom Operator* network at any time if it determines, in its sole discretion, that the connection may be being used for purposes other than the business, or that the Village Phone Operator is not complying with the terms of this Agreement, the terms of the *Village Phone Operator Manual* or the terms of the loan agreement. It is recorded that *Village Phone Company* has reserved for itself the right in its agreement with the microfinance institution, to which agreement this Agreement is subject, to temporarily or permanently disconnect the SIM from the *Telecom Operator* network if its agreement with the microfinance institution terminates or at any time if it determines, in its sole discretion, that the connection may be being used for purposes other than the business, or that the Village Phone Operator is not complying with the terms of this Agreement or the terms of the *Village Phone Operator Manual.*

3.3   In the event that the Village Phone Operator fails to comply with the terms of this Agreement and the *Village Phone Operator Manual,* the microfinance institution shall be entitled to immediately, without notice, terminate this Agreement.

3.4   This Agreement will, unless terminated in terms of clause 3.3, endure indefinitely until terminated by either party on no less than thirty (30) days written notice to the other party.

3.5   If this Agreement terminates, the microfinance institution shall be entitled to disconnect the SIM from the *Telecom Operator* network. The Village Phone Operator shall also return any signs or marketing collateral containing a *Telecom Operator* or *Village Phone Company* trademark to the microfinance institution. This obligation shall survive termination of this Agreement.

3.6   The Village Phone Operator shall not be entitled to cede or assign the right to use the SIM or carry on the business or any other rights recorded in this Agreement to any other person.

3.7   The Village Phone Operator acknowledges that all risk of loss, damage, wear and tear or destruction of the phone and SIM shall be borne by the Village Phone Operator save to the extent that it is able to claim under a warranty provided by the manufacturer. Should any of the above events occur, it shall be the responsibility of the Village Phone Operator to claim directly from the manufacturer under the warranty or replace the damaged, destroyed or worn out equipment at the Village Phone Operator's own cost, and it shall be in the discretion of the microfinance institution as to whether it will be prepared to advance further loans to the Village Phone Operator for this purpose. The Village Phone Operator is responsible for proper care, maintenance and repair of the phone and the SIM at all times.

3.8   The Village Phone Operator undertakes to comply in all respects with the microfinance institution's directions, from time to time, concerning the operation of the business and the use of the SIM.

3.9   The Village Phone Operator acknowledges that it is subject to the standard conditions of service of *Village Phone Company* contained in the starter pack. *Village*

Phone Company has instructed the microfinance institution to advise the Village Phone Operator, as it hereby does, that the special tariffs afforded to the Village Phone Operator pursuant to this Agreement will be published to the Village Phone Operator by *Village Phone Company* from time to time by publication to the microfinance institution and that they shall be subject to variation by *Village Phone Company* as set out in the standard conditions of service.

3.10   All notices in connection with this Agreement shall be sent to the respective addresses of the parties referred to above.

SIGNED AT_____ON_____20_____

Village Phone Operator

SIGNED AT_____ON_____20_____

Microfinance Institution

FOR OFFICE USE ONLY	
TELEPHONE NUMBER ALLOCATED TO THE VILLAGE PHONE OPERATOR	
SIM SERIAL NUMBER	
TELEPHONE SERIAL NUMBER	

APPENDIX D: VILLAGE PHONE OPERATOR MANUAL FOR VILLAGE PHONE

Note: This is available as a separate document if needed.

PROGRAM MANUAL FOR VILLAGE PHONE OPERATORS

Version: Template V1.0

1.0 WELCOME

Congratulations on becoming a Village Phone Operator! This is a fantastic opportunity for you and your community.

You have been selected as a Village Phone Operator because your microfinance organization has recommended you based upon your relationship and history with them.

This document will help you understand how to operate your phone business and some of the most important requirements and responsibilities.

2.0 OBLIGATIONS OF A VILLAGE PHONE OPERATOR

2.1 Business Obligations

As a Village Phone Operator, you are a vital resource for your community, providing a service for everyone. Owning this business comes with certain responsibilities and obligations:

Your phone business must operated so that the members of your community always have access to the phone service. Although you may locate the phone business where you see the best business opportunity, this should be predictable and people should be able to rely upon your service.

The phone must be **available for use 24 hours per day, 7 days per week.** People will grow dependent on your services to access information and communicate with other people. If there is an emergency, someone should be able to use the phone no matter what time of day or night.

In your community, **everyone must have access** to the phone. You cannot deny use of the phone unless a person does not want to pay for the services.

A **sign must be posted** advertising the availability of the Village Phone. A sign is included as part of the Starter Kit. You should never pay taxes on your signpost. Please contact your microfinance institution if you are asked to pay taxes by local authorities.

The phone **cannot move outside of your village for personal use**. If you travel for personal business, you cannot take the phone with you; if you travel to another new village, you must leave the phone behind.

The **business and phone are not transferable**. If you no longer wish to operate a Village Phone business, you must return the phone, *Village Phone Company* marketing materials (e.g. sign post and marketing cards) and/or SIM card to your microfinance institution.

The phone will be **operated only by the Village Phone Operator or a family member**. The microfinance field officer should be given the names of the family members who will be assisting in running the business. *[Village Phone Operator businesses are often operated by an employee of the owner – you should determine your own policy on this]*

You **must charge the tariffs listed** on the tariff sheet for use of the phone. Additional services can be created and billed at your discretion.

A **call log will be maintained** and made available to your MFI field officer and *Village Phone Company* staff. A call log template can be seen in *Appendix B*.

Until completion of the loan agreement, the **microfinance institution will retain ownership** of all equipment supplied under this agreement.

The **SIM card connection always remains the property of the microfinance institution** and can be disconnected by *Telecom Operator* upon request from the microfinance institution. The sign post and marketing materials always remain property of your microfinance organization.

The **Village Phone Operator is responsible for proper care**, maintenance and repair of the equipment at all times.

The **Village Phone Operator is responsible for any lost or stolen equipment**. All financial obligations will continue in such a situation.

If the equipment is stolen, the Village Phone Operator will be required to make a **report to the police** station and get the appropriate report from the police so that the necessary actions can be made by the *Telecom Operator* to block the phone.

Upon **death of the Village Phone Operator**, a family member has the option to join the microfinance institution and continue the business in the place of the deceased member. If this option is not exercised, the SIM and equipment must be returned to the microfinance institution. If ownership of the equipment has been transferred to the Village Phone Operator by virtue of completion of the financial obligation, then this is retained by the family (except the SIM card connection and Village Phone branded marketing materials).

Throughout the course of business operation, the **Village Phone Operator must remain a member of the microfinance institution** (maintain a loan or savings) and shall attend regular meetings. If this membership lapses, the Village Phone Operator forfeits the right to operate a Village Phone business and the SIM card shall be deactivated.

It is only possible for a Village Phone Operator to own one Village Phone. *[This policy may change – this will go back to the balance in your mission as to two complementary goals: 1. The creation of entrepreneur owned and operated Village Phone Operator businesses, and 2. Serving as many people as possible.]*

Airtime shall be **purchased only from the microfinance institution.** *[This policy may change]*

2.2 Understanding the Loan

Your microfinance field officer will explain the details of your loan to you when you sign your loan agreement. In particular, you should be sure that you understand the following elements:

- Grace period for the loan
- Total loan amount and cost for all the equipment in the Starter Kit
- Loan duration
- Amount for each loan payment
- Loan period
- Frequency of repayments

There will be a summary of this information on the Village Phone Deployment Record document you sign when you receive your Equipment Starter kit.

The collateral for your loan is the phone and other equipment. If the phone is lost or stolen, you are responsible for replacing it. All non-warranty repair expenses are the responsibility of the Village Phone Operator.

The loan is for the equipment only, not the SIM card connection in the phone. The SIM card connection remains the property of the Telecom Operator.

If you have any questions or do not understand any of these items, be sure to talk to your microfinance field officer.

3.0 EQUIPMENT

3.1 Contents of the Village Phone Starter Kit

The Village Phone Starter Kit contains everything necessary to begin operating a Village Phone business. The kit contains:

- A Samsung R220 mobile phone with battery.
- Owner's Manual for the phone. The manual gives detailed instructions about the use of the mobile phone.
- Plastic case with SIM card and airtime cards. The SIM card should already have been installed (it goes inside the phone and makes it operate). The airtime cards are like money. When you enter their numbers into the mobile phone, you increase the balance of the account on your phone. As long as you have a positive balance in the account on your phone, you can make and receive calls.
- Village Phone sign. You can put this sign up to show everybody that you have a mobile phone they can use to make phone calls.
- Marketing cards. These cards should include your name, location and phone number and be distributed to friends and family so they can call you or share with others to further distribute your phone number.
- Antenna with cable and adapter to connect it to the phone. The antenna improves the quality of the phone call and will let you hear other people's voices better.
- Village Phone Operator Manual.

Optionally, there may also be equipment to recharge the battery in the phone. Depending on your location and requirements, this will be either a solar panel with cable and adapter to connect it to the phone or an automobile battery with adapter.

If any of the items are missing or broken, please contact your microfinance field officer.

3.2 Connecting the Equipment

Connecting the Antenna

The first thing you need to do is to connect the antenna to the mobile phone so that you can make the best quality phone calls. The steps to take are:

1. Connect the long, heavy cable to the antenna (if not already connected).
2. Connect the small adapter cable to the heavy cable.
3. On the back of the mobile phone, find the small rubber plug in the upper-left. Remove this rubber plug to reveal a silver connector.
4. Connect the other end of the adapter cable into the phone. Important: The connector between the adapter cable and the phone breaks very easily. Always leave the adapter cable plugged into the phone. If you need to disconnect the phone, disconnect the adapter cable from the large antenna cable, leaving the adapter cable connected to the phone.

Aiming and Mounting the Antenna

It is important the antenna is pointed in the best direction to get the highest possible signal. To do this:

1. Turn on the phone by pressing the red power button.
2. Look at the signal strength indicator in the upper-left corner of the display. There can be up to six bars displayed.
3. Have someone hold the antenna vertically (with the short ends pointing towards the ground).
4. Aim the antenna in the direction of the nearest *Telecom Operator* base station or repeater. These are usually located in towns or trading centers.
5. Watch the signal strength indicator and determine which direction has the strongest signal (the most bars).
6. Attach the antenna on top of a tall object such as a pole. You want the antenna to be as high as possible, at least 10m from the ground, and not blocking the "line of sight" to the nearest base station.
7. Point the antenna in the direction that gives the best signal strength.
8. Secure antenna several places (e.g. in the ground, and in the middle to a building, or supporting post).

3.3 Charging the Batteries

Reliable Power Source

The Samsung R220 phone comes with a standard Li-ion battery. A fully charged battery will allow up to 6 hours of talk time and up to 150 hours of "standby" time.

When you open your starter kit, you should immediately start charging the phone. The initial charge for the battery will take approximately three hours. You can see how much energy is in the battery by looking at the battery meter on the right side of the display on the phone.

It is important to only charge your phone from a reliable power source. Gasoline powered generators are an inconsistent source of power and can destroy the battery or the phone. Some villages have consistent power fluctuations that can damage electrical appliances. If you know that your village has this problem then you must always charge your phone from a power source supplied with your phone. If you fail to observe these guidelines you may risk destroying your phone or battery and will have to purchase a new one at your own expense.

Installing and using the solar panel

Place the solar panel in a location where it will receive as much direct sunlight as possible (for example, on the roof of a building).

The phone can be recharged by plugging the recharging cable into the receptacle attached to the solar panel. The phone should be connected to the solar panel as much as possible during daytime so that the energy from the sun can recharge the batteries. It should be disconnected after 5:00pm and not reconnected before 7:00am

Using an automobile battery

It is also possible to recharge the mobile phone by connecting it to a car battery. Connect the clamps of the adapter cable to the battery and plug in the car charger to the adapter. You will observe that the red light on the adapter cable is on when the cables are connected properly ("+" to red, "-"to black). You can then connect the car charger to your phone. You will observe that the phone is charging when the small battery in the upper right corner of the phone screen is moving. When this indicator stops moving your phone is fully charged and you should disconnect it from the battery. Your car battery needs to be recharged every two months to prevent it from becoming defective.

IMPORTANT: Be sure to match the symbols on the clips to the symbols on the battery. The "+" clip (RED) must connect to the "+" terminal and the "-" clip (BLACK) must connect to the "-" terminal.

A battery charging log is included at the end of this manual (Appendix E). It is a good idea to record the date you charge your car battery to ensure that you charge it before it is completely discharged.

3.4 Warranty Information

Samsung phone and battery

Your Samsung R220 phone comes with a one year warranty. Details for this warranty can be found in the Samsung documentation in the starter kit and should be read carefully by the Village Phone Operator. In general the warranty will cover manufacturing problems with the phone, but it will *not* cover damage to the phone. For example, if you drop the phone and it breaks, repair would not be covered under the warranty. The battery is *not* covered by a warranty.

If you believe there to be a manufacturing defect, in order to return the phone and take advantage of the warranty you must have the box and all the original parts that came with the phone. Please take care to save the box in case you need to return the phone during the warranty period.

Any warranty repair for the phone must happen at the authorized service center noted below, and as the owner of the phone you must take it to the service center yourself. Any unauthorized repair voids the warranty. To repair the phone, contact:

Your local authorized repair dealer

Name

Address

Phone

Email

Solar panels

The solar panel comes with a warranty against manufacturing defects for one year. In the event of a problem with your solar panel, contact:

> Your local authorized repair dealer
>
> Name
>
> Address
>
> Phone
>
> Email

Batteries

For warranty issues, take to the nearest authorized UBL dealer with warranty card for service.

> Your local authorized repair dealer
>
> Name
>
> Address
>
> Phone
>
> Email

Antennas and Patch Cords

If one of these items appears damaged, the Village Phone Operator should contact the Customer Service Help-Line on [Phone Number]. Then if further assistance is needed, contact their microfinance institution. If damage is a manufacturing defect, the item will be replaced. If damaged from negligence (knowingly breaking the equipment), the Village Phone Operator will be required to purchase a replacement item.

3.5 Using the Phone

[Customize for your selected Phone handset]

The Samsung R220 phone is a full featured mobile phone. This section includes basic information to help you get started using the phone for your Village Phone business. Please refer to the Samsung documentation that accompanies your phone for explanations about the different features of the phone. Please also see Appendix I. Points to Remember.

Making a Domestic Call

Dialing someone in-country is very simple. Simply enter the phone number and press the green call button. When you are finished, press the red button to end the call.

The first three numbers of the phone number indicate which system the phone you are calling is on. There are different charges for calls to each of these different systems. See the tariff sheet in *Appendix A* for rate details.

Examples Village Phone Operator Training Outline At Deployment and Establishment of a NEW Village Phone Business	
077, 03X, 078	MTN
04X	UTL
071	Mango
075	Celtel

International calls

Within East Africa (Kenya, Tanzania, Rwanda or Burundi: Enter one of the following dialing codes: 005 (Kenya); 007 (Tanzania); 0037 (Rwanda); and 0038 (Burundi).

To call all other international destinations: First enter a "+" before the number. Press and hold down the"0" key and the "+" will appear.

After the "+" you enter the "international dialing code" for the country you are calling and the phone number. For example, +1 12 345678 (1 is the international dialing code for the United States)

A detailed list of all international dialing codes is in Appendix F. If you have trouble placing an international call, or are unsure of the international code please call the Village Phone Customer Service Help-Line and request assistance.

See the Tariff Sheet, Appendix A for rate details.

Timing a call

The Samsung phone has a built-in timer which will tell you how many minutes each phone call lasted. You will use this information to determine how much to charge your customers. To see the last call time, press the Menu button (on the upper-left part of the phone, above the green phone button). Then press the numbers 1-4. For example:

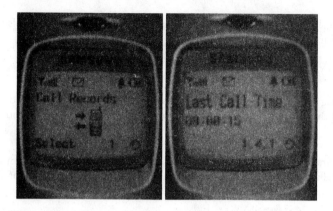

Purchasing and checking airtime

[Customize]

You cannot place any phone calls until you have loaded airtime into your phone. The Starter Kit comes with your first airtime card. To load this airtime, follow the instructions on the card (call 155 and enter the airtime card information or enter *156* followed by the access number and then press "#").

You should always purchase airtime from your microfinance institution. Be sure to always have enough airtime on your phone to be able to operate your business for at least two weeks. Call *156# to check how much airtime is remaining on your phone.

4.0 RUNNING YOUR VILLAGE PHONE BUSINESS

A Village Phone Operator earns money by selling the use of the mobile phone to members of the community. The price that the Village Phone Operator charges customers is higher than the price paid for the airtime.

A Village Phone Operator earns money in two ways:

1. The basic retail margin is *[Margin]* per minute *[or Unit]* for all domestic calls. So, for a five minute call to a *Telecom Operator* phone number, the Village Phone Operator makes at least *[Calculate]*.
2. 2)   A Village Phone Operator may also charge for additional services, such as traveling to tell an individual they have received a call. Pricing and definition of these services is at the discretion of the Village Phone Operator.

4.1 Charging for calls

The Village Phone Operator is only charged for outgoing calls. The Village Phone Operator should charge the user of the phone by timing the length of the call and rounding up to the nearest minute. For example:

- 1:53 phone call to *[Other Operator 1]* number will be charged for 2 minutes *[Example]*
- 2:07 phone call to *[Other Operator 2]* number will be charged for 3 minutes *[Example]*

There is no charge to the Village Phone Operator for incoming calls. Beeping has been disabled for all Village Phones *[Comment: To avoid zero revenue calls for Village Phone Operators]*. When you place a call, the recipient will not see your phone number.

All customers must pay for their calls with cash. Do not extend credit to any of your customers. You can say, "Yes, you are my friend, but to my business you are my customer".

4.2 Contacting Customer Support

If you are having difficulty with your phone, please contact the Village Phone Customer Service Help-Line by dialing *[Phone Number]*.

The helpline is open 24 hours a day, Monday to Sunday – but the best time to call is between 8AM and 10PM. *[Customize]* They can assist you with any problems related to network, the antenna, the car battery, or your phone. This is a free call and the Village Phone Customer Service Help-Line can only be accessed from Village Phones. If you cannot use the phone, please contact your microfinance field officer who will try to help you.

4.3 SMS Messages and Additional Services

In addition to using the mobile phone for voice phone calls, you can also use the phone to send and receive text information. This can be a very efficient way to send and receive short messages and is also an efficient way of retrieving important information such as commodity prices and foreign exchange rates. See *Appendix H* for step-by-step instructions on how to send SMS messages to retrieve information.

Email messages can also be sent to your phone. Your email address is: *[Customize]*

4.4 Financial Analysis- Making a Profit

The rate charged by *the Telecom Operator* for each minute of airtime varies depending on the phone number that is called, day and the time. However, the rate you charge your customers does *not* change based on time or day of the week.

4.5 Keeping a Phone Log

You must keep a log of all of your business activity. The date of call, duration of call, system called, outgoing/incoming/service, and amount charged are all important pieces of information. Customer information is also useful. For example:

Call Date	Duration	Network	Business Income			
			Outgoing Charges (A)	Incoming charges (B)	SMS Charges (C)	Charges (A+B+C+D)
17-Feb	2:43	Example	1200	0	0	1200

You should acquire a call log book and create columns to keep a log like that shown in *Appendix B.* Your microfinance institution loan officer and Village Phone staff will periodically come to your business and ask to review your log book.

4.6 Marketing your business

It is very important for people in your community to know about your business. There is a sign in the starter kit. Post the sign prominently to advertise your Village Phone business. You will also receive a number of Village Phone business cards to distribute to customers (and for them to give to their family and friends so they know your phone number). *Appendix G* provides some useful ideas on how to distribute your business cards.

5.0 FREQUENTLY ASKED QUESTIONS AND ISSUES

5.1 What Happens If...

- **...the phone is lost or stolen:** Report the event to police and to the microfinance field officer at your microfinance institution so that the phone can be blocked. It is also best to file a police report, and provide your microfinance institution and *Village Phone Company* with copies.
- **...I move to another village:** You must check with your microfinance field officer to see if you can take the Village Phone business to the new village. If your new village is outside the *Telecom Operator* service area, you will need to forfeit the business.
- **...the phone stops working:** First, following the instructions in the "Solving Problems" section of the Samsung Phone Owner's manual. If you are unsuccessful, call the Village Phone Customer Service Help-Line for assistance. If that does not work, you can try asking friends or your microfinance field officer. The final option is to take the phone to a Service

Center. Do **NOT** try to repair the phone yourself. Opening the phone voids the warranty.

- **...I want to sell or transfer the business.** The business can not be sold or transferred. If you would like to cease operations, notify your microfinance field officer.
- **...a Village Phone Operator dies**: The first option is to transfer the business to another family member who must join the microfinance group and be an active member. Alternatively, the business will be forfeited, and the SIM card and *Village Phone Company* branded marketing materials (sign post and marketing cards) must be returned to the microfinance institution.

5.2 Operational Tips

Some useful suggestions for operating your Village Phone Business:

- **Maintain an airtime buffer, at least *[One week of expected usage – expressed in currency terms]*.** If you run out of airtime, you cannot operate your business. Be sure to regularly monitor your airtime balance and purchase an airtime card from your microfinance field officer long before you run out. You can check your airtime balance by dialing *[Phone Number]*.
- **Do not let other people dial the phone.** It is easy for someone to change the settings on your phone (either deliberately or accidentally). Since the phone is yours, insist that your customers simply use it to talk.
- **If the battery is low, leave the charger plugged in while talking**. As long as the phone is connected to a power source, it will continue to charge, even if it is being used.
- **Avoid overcharging the battery**. If the phone is fully charged, do not leave it plugged into the power source.
- **Use the call timer built into the phone.** The Samsung phone automatically times each call. You can see the duration of the last call by pressing menu-1-4-1.
- **Never divert calls.** This would allow somebody else to receive your phone calls.
- **Voicemail is an option.** If the phone is in use when someone calls your number, they have the option of leaving a voicemail message. You can retrieve their message by dialing *[Phone Number]*. You are charged for this call to retrieve your messages, so use this feature with caution.

5.3 Additional Questions and Answers

How do I load a Pay-as-you-Go card?

[Customize]

For example: "Simply scratch the silver panel of your Pay as you Go card to reveal the secret access number. Then dial [Phone Number] from your phone. When you're welcomed to the service, press [Number] . Then enter your access number followed by #. The system will repeat the access number to you – if it is correct, press [Number]. You are now connected! "

How can I check my airtime balance?

Simply type *[Code Number]* onto your handset then press the calling button. The balance will appear on your screen.

How can I find my Handset's serial number?

Type *[Code Number]* onto your phone.

I have just received an SMS. How can I read it?

1. Access the menu on your handset.
2. Scroll through the menu and look for the 'Messages' or an equivalent icon.
3. The 'Message' icon should have its own sub menu.
4. One of these sub menus should be 'Read Messages' or 'Read'
5. Provided that you have received an SMS, choosing the 'Read Message' or 'Read' option will open and display your SMS.
6. If you have more than one SMS you will be able to access them via the 'Read Message' function.
7. Your phone will only hold up to 10 SMSs. You will need to delete old unwanted messages to make room for new messages.

TARIFF SHEET

The charges to customers for use of the phone are as follows:

[Insert your customer (retail) tariff sheet here]

CALL LOG

VPO Name _____

VPO Phone Number _____

Call Date	Duration	Network	Business Income			
			Outgoing charges (A)	Incoming charges (B)	SMS charges (C)	Charges (A+B+C+D)
17-Feb	2:43	Example	1200	0	0	1200

SAMPLE RETAIL MARGINS

. Margins for a Village Phone Operator based on the destination:

[Insert Village Phone Operator Margins here – this may vary according to time of day, geographic destination, network destination, etc... You should also include a Weighted Average Village Phone Operator Margin (Blended) based upon historic calling patterns for rural users]

IMPORTANT PHONE NUMBERS

Name	Number

BATTERY CHARGING LOG

Date   Phone
Received

Charging Date	Location of Charging Station	Comments

INTERNATIONAL DIALING CODES

Country	Intl dial code	Country	Intl dial code	Country	Intl dial code
Albania	355	Guatemala	502	Palestine	970
Algeria	213	Guinea Bissau	245	Panama	507
Andorra	376	Guinea Republic	224	Papua New Guinea	675
Angola	244	Guyana	592	Paraguay	595
Anguilla	264	Haiti	509	Peru	51
Antigua and Barbuda	268	Honduras	503	Philippines	63
Argentina	54	Hong Kong	852	Poland	48
Armenia	374	Hungary	36	Portugal	351
Aruba	297	Iceland	354	Puerto Rico	787
Ascension Island	247	India	91	Qatar	974
Australia	61	Indonesia	62	Reunion Island	262
Austria	43	Iran	98	Romania	40
Azerbaijan	994	Iraq	964	Russia	7
Bahamas	242	Ireland	353	Rwanda	250
Bahrain	973	Israel	972	Samoa (American)	684
Bangladesh	880	Italy	39	Samoa (Western)	685
Barbados	246	Ivory Coast	225	San Marino	378
Belarus	375	Jamaica	876	Sao Tome & Principe	239
Belgium	32	Japan	81	Saudi Arabia	966
Belize	501	Jordan	962	Senegal	221
Benin	229	Kazakhstan	7	Serbia	381
Bermuda	441	Kenya	254	Seychelles	248
Bhutan	975	Kiribati	686	Sierra Leone	232
Bolivia	591	Korea, North	850	Singapore	65
Bosnia	387	Korea, South	82	Slovak Republic	421
Botswana	267	Kuwait	965	Slovenia	386
Brazil	55	Kyrgyzstan	996	Solomon Islands	677
Brunei	673	Laos	856	Somalia	252
Bulgaria	359	Latvia	371	South Africa	27
Burkina Faso	226	Lebanon	961	Spain	34
Burundi	257	Lesotho	266	Sri Lanka	94

continued

Central Africa Republic	236	Liberia	231	St Helena	290
Chad	235	Libya	218	St Kitts & Nevia	869
Chile	56	Liechtenstein	423	St Lucia	758
China	86	Lithuania	370	Sudan	249
Columbia	57	Luxembourg	352	Surinam	597
Comoros Island	269	Macao	853	Swaziland	268
Congo	242	Macedonia (Fyrom)	389	Sweden	46
Cook Islands	682	Madagascar	261	Switzerland	41
Costa Rica	506	Malawi	265	Syria	963
Croatia	385	Malaysia	60	Taiwan	886
Cuba	53	Maldives Republic	960	Tajikistan	992
Cyprus	357	Mali	223	Tanzania	255
Czech Republic	420	Malta	356	Thailand	66
Democratic Republic of Congo (Zaire)	243	Mariana Islands	670	The Gambia	220
Denmark	45	Marshall Islands	692	Togo	228
Diego Garcia	246	Martinique	596	Tonga	676
Djibouti	253	Mauritius	230	Trinidad & Tobago	868
Dominica Islands	767	Mayotte Islands	269	Tunisia	216
Dominican Republic	809	Mexico	52	Turkey	90
Ecuador	593	Micronesia	691	Turkmenistan	993
Egypt	20	Moldova	373	Turks & Caicos Islands	649
El Salvador	503	Monaco	377	Tuvalu	688
Equatorial Guinea	240	Mongolia	976	Uganda	256
Eritrea	291	Montserrat	664	Ukraine	380
Estonia	372	Morocco	212	United Arab Emirates	971

continued

Ethiopia	251	Mozambique	258	United Kingdom	44
Faeroe Islands	298	Myanmar (Burma)	95	Uruguay	598
Falkland Islands	500	Namibia	264	USA	1
Fiji Islands	679	Nauru	674	Uzbekistan	998
Finland	358	Nepal	977	Vanuatu	678
France	33	Netherlands	31	Venezuela	58
French Guiana	594	Netherlands Antilles	599	Vietnam	84
French Polynesia	689	New Caledonia	687	Wallis & Futuna Islands	681
Gabon	241	New Zealand	64	Yemen Arab Republic	967
Georgia	995	Nicaragua	505	Zambia	260
Germany	49	Niger	227	Zimbabwe	263
Ghana	233	Nigeria	234		
Gibraltar	350	Niue Island	683		
Greece	30	Norfolk Island	672		
Greenland	299	Norway	47		
Grenada	473	Oman	968		
Guadeloupe	590	Pakistan	92		
Guam	671	Palau	680		

BUSINESS CARD DISTRIBUTION POINTERS

Fill out the information boxes on the back of your cards with your name, the address where your phone is located, and your Village Phone number.

- Give out your cards to local leaders, community members and clients who regularly use your Village Phone.
- Distribute cards at local churches, mosques, hospitals and schools.
- Give out cards to relatives and friends in other towns and Villages, and during market days.
- The more people who know about your Village Phone the more clients you will receive and the more money you will make

HOW TO USE ADDITIONAL MENU FEATURES

[Any network specific SIM programmed extra features should be discussed here]

POINTS TO REMEMBER

[One Page Summary of Key Points]

REFERENCE GUIDE

(Sample from Rwanda):

MAKING CALLS

To dial someone in country
1. Enter the phone number
2. Press the green call button. When finished, press the red button to end the call.

To dial someone in East Africa
1. Enter the calling prefix for the country you are calling
2. Enter the phone number
3. Press the green call button. When finished, press the red button to end the call

For example, to dial the number 8312345678 in Kenya you would enter "**071**8312345678" on the phone and then press the green button.

To dial all other international numbers
1. Press and hold down the "0" key until a "+" appears
2. Enter the international dialing code for the country you are calling (see other side of this sheet)
3. Enter the phone number
4. Press the green call button. When finished, press the red button to end the call

CHECKING AIRTIME BALANCE
1. Type *110# onto your handset
2. Press the green calling button. The balance will appear on your screen.

TO LOAD AIRTIME
1. Press *111*
2. Enter the number on the airtime card
3. Press #
4. Press green calling button

TO CHECK LAST CALL TIME
Press Menu then 1 and 4.

TO READ MESSAGES
Press Menu then 2 and 2.

TO SEND A MESSAGE
Press Menu then 2 and 3.

TO VIEW A MISSED CALL
Press Menu then press 1.

TO STORE A NEW NUMBER
Type number e.g. 039 123456, press save then type name e.g. John then press save.

TO FIND PHONE NUMBER ALREADY IN THE PHONE

Press phonebook, then ok. Press, find entry and type the first letter of name and then search.

CALL TARIFFS

Destination (Service or Country)	Charge per unit*
To MTN	20
RwandaTel	25
East Africa (Kenya, Tanzania, Uganda, Burundi, DR Congo)	50
All other international	70
SMS	55
MTN Services	65

* Units are 8 seconds long. See the call tariffs chart to determine what to charge based on the length of the call.

EAST AFRICA CALLING PREFIXES

Country	Calling prefix
Kenya	071
Tanzania	074
Uganda	070
Burundi	072
D.R. Congo	073

REMEMBER!

- Only charge your phone using the battery and cables supplied with the phone. Never hook your phone up to a generator – it will ruin the phone.
- The phone MUST always remain in a fixed location
- The phone MUST be available to the public 24 hours, 7 days a week
- You MUST only charge the tariff rates listed on the signpost.
- All airtime cards MUST be purchased from your MFI
- You MUST remain a member of the MFI to retain the SIM card for your phone
- You are responsible for all lost or stolen equipment
- Always maintain a call log for all calls made through your phone.
- The sign post MUST be displayed outside your operating location
- Market your business – give business cards to friends, family and colleagues; give them out at churches, mosques, trading centers, and other places
- Maintain an airtime buffer, at least 3,500 RWF
- Do not let other people dial the phone
- If the battery is low, leave the charger plugged in while talking.

Contact Customer Service

Call 454 Toll Free

APPENDIX E: OPERATIONS MANUAL OUTLINE FOR VILLAGE PHONE COMPANY

1.0 INTRODUCTION

1.1 Institutional Background

1.2 Incorporation

1.3 Village Phone Stakeholders

- Catalyst
- Telecom Operator
- Microfinance Institutions (MFIs) - "The Market Channel"
- Village Phone Operators –"The Retailer"

1.4 Stakeholder Agreements

1.5 Operations Documents

The following table lists documents utilized in the operation of Village Phone Company:

Operational Document	Content Summary
Microfinance Institution Manual	- Business Model - Village Phone Operator selection - Application, approval and deployment process - Monitoring, evaluation and reporting
Village Phone Operator Manual	- Obligations of a Village Phone Operator - Understanding the loan - Operating the equipment - Running the business
Village Phone Company Operations Manual (this document)	- Operational and Business partners - Operational structures - Procedures
Helpdesk Training Manual	- Details most frequently cited problems and questions put to Helpdesk - Provides information and solutions to be used so Helpdesk staff (Customer Care) can respond to queries

2.0 ORGANIZATIONAL STRUCTURE

The following graphic illustrates the roles and responsibilities for each of the partners in Village Phone Company

3.0 PLANNING FOR DEPLOYMENT

3.1 Strategic Planning

- Network Planning
- Deployment Forecasting

3.2 Designation of Village Phone Operators

- Identification and Application
- Approval

3.3 Equipment Procurement

- Inventory

Product in Starter Kit	Current Supplier	Critical Attributes	Desired Warranty	Price Range
Mobile handset				
Car chargers				
Fixed battery clips				
Car batteries				
Solar panels				
High gain antennas				
Antenna extension cable				
Patch cords				
SIM Kit (coded SIM chip, airtime card, phone manuals)				
Sign/Tariff Board				

The process for managing inventory is as follows:

Order process for microfinance institution

Equipment Pick-up

Loading the SIM card

3.4 Training and Deployment

- MFI Training
- VPO Training and Deployment

4.0 BUSINESS SERVICE AND SUPPORT

4.1 Operator Activities

- Obligations of the VPO
- Temporary and Permanent blocks on phones

4.2 Call Centre

4.3 Airtime

- Airtime
- SIM Card

4.4 Warranty and Repair

4.5 SMS

4.6 MFI Incentive Program

5.0 MARKETING

5.1 Branding and Positioning

5.2 Interaction with Government

6.0 ADMINISTRATION

6.1 Finance

- Business Plan
- Budget
- Finance Administration

6.2 Information Technology

- General Support
- Data Maintenance
- Reports

6.3 Legal

- Contracts and Legal Documents
- Confidentiality and Disclosure of Information
- The Board

6.4 Miscellaneous Administration Needs

- Office space and facilities
- Telephony
- Cars
- Travel

7.0 HUMAN RESOURCES

7.1 Recruitment

7.2 Remuneration and Benefits

7.3 Performance Management

7.4 Disciplinary Code

8.0 MONITORING AND REPORTING

APPENDIX A: SCHEDULE OF FORMS

APPENDIX B: KEY CONTACTS

- Telecom Operator
- Operations
- Human resources
- Finance
- Marketing
- Mapping and Planning
- Customer Care
- Distribution Center
- Customer Support
- Suppliers

- Microfinance Institutions
- Donor Organizations
- Potential Partners
- Government Partners

APPENDIX C: NETWORK COVERAGE

APPENDIX D: MFI DEPLOYMENT PLAN

APPENDIX E: Village Phone Company ORDER FORM

APPENDIX F: TRIP PLANNING REPORT

APPENDIX G: DOMESTIC TRAVEL REQUISITION

APPENDIX H: FIELD REPORT

APPENDIX I: AIRTIME BALANCES AND SERVICE FEE EXPIRATIONS

APPENDIX J: VPO CALL MONITORING

APPENDIX K: ACCOUNTABILITY FOR IMPREST ADVANCE

APPENDIX L: DEPLOYMENT RECORD

APPENDIX M: FIELD VISIT CHECK LIST

APPENDIX N: VEHICLE CONDITION FORM

APPENDIX O: FREQUENTLY ASKED QUESTIONS ABOUT Village Phone

APPENDIX P: STAFF PERFORMANCE AND DEVELOPMENT REVIEW

APPENDIX F: HELP LINE REFERENCE MANUAL TEMPLATE

Note: This is available as a separate document if needed.

HELPLINE
REFERENCE MANUAL

Version: Template V1.0

THE HELPLINE REFERENCE MANUAL

This manual is designed as a training and reference tool for the team of helpline operators who will serve the network of Village Phone Operators. This document is not intended for broad distribution with the Village Phone program and is not for Village Phone Operators or for MFIs.

1.0 INTRODUCTION TO VILLAGEPHONE

1.1 Grameen's Village Phone Program- Success in Poverty Reduction

One of the greatest success stories in international development has been Grameen's Village Phone Program in Bangladesh. In rural villages where no telecommunications service has previously existed, cellular phones are provided to very poor women who use the phone to operate a business providing communications services to her community. At the close of 2000, there were 3273 Village Phones deployed. By mid 2004, there were over 70,000 Village Phones deployed in poor rural villages of Bangladesh. Airtime usage per phone has also increased and is on average more than five times that for an urban phone.

The most obvious benefit of the Village Phone program is the economic impact that telecommunications access brings to the entire village/parish. There is clear evidence of this impact from Bangladesh, including higher prices paid to Village Phone users for their agricultural produce or manufactured goods and better exchange rates when repatriating funds. For the cost of a phone call, a family is able to save the expense of sending a productive member to deliver or retrieve information by traveling great distances in person.

> *"Farmers from the villages use the phones to call the city markets to find out prices for their produce. Previously they were a little bit short-changed by their middlemen. The middlemen would say a lower price than what the actual market price was. So now they can call the market themselves to find out what the actual price of eggs or whatever their produce is. An independent study found that half the people who use the phones regularly, traders in rice or bananas for example, make more money from their business and they save 10 hours in travel time."*

> *"If the Grameen Telecom experience is a reliable guide, then providing phone service yields powerful social and economic benefits in rural communities….Empowering poor communities by providing a wide range of digitally enabled self-help tools – via the private sector – could become a crucial part of an effective rural development strategy … Business is a proven method of solving their [the poor] problems in a sustainable way."*

In a Canadian International Development Agency (CIDA) commissioned study, it was concluded that the Grameen Village Phone program yields "significant positive social and economic impacts, including relatively large consumer surplus and immeasurable quality of life benefits". The study concluded that the consumer surplus for a single phone call ranges from 2.64% to 9.8% of mean monthly household income. The cost of a trip to the city ranges from two to eight times the cost of a single phone call, meaning that the real savings for poor rural people is between $2.70 and $10.00 for individual calls. The income that Village Phone Operators derive from the Village Phone is about 24% of the household income on average – in some cases it was as high as 40% of the household income.

Most critically, Village Phone Operators become socially and economically empowered. Some creative and entrepreneurial users of the technology identify new business opportunities, including the resale of information to others in their communities. The technology also serves to link regional entrepreneurs with each other and their clients, bringing more business to small enterprises. Grameen's experience in Bangladesh has shown that information technology has enormous potential for increasing local economic activity and business opportunities.

Because the phone operators are typically female and the phones are in their places of business, women who might otherwise have very limited access to a phone feel comfortable using one. Furthermore, as these phones become so important for the whole village, the status of women in the communities where they work is enhanced.

> *"Phones have helped elevate the status of the female phone operators in the village. Surveys have found that the Village Phone Operators become socially empowered as they earn an income, gaining participation in family decisions in which, in rural Bangladeshi society, women usually have no say."*

> *"… [Grameen Village Phone] has had considerable development benefits. It has reduced the cost of communications relative to other services such as transportation….the program has enabled the village pay phone entrepreneurs, poor by most standards but among the better-off in their villages, to turn a profit."*

Having established the infrastructure and institutional framework for such a venture, the poor become the drivers of their own destiny and the experts in the utilization of this technology to their own best advantages – telecommunications is a powerful catalyst and facilitator of such grassroots, self directed development :

> *"Isolation and lack of information [communications] are very serious obstacles to poverty eradication"*

> *"People lack many things: jobs, shelter, food, health care and drinkable water. Today, being cut off from basic telecommunications services is a hardship almost as acute as these other deprivations, and may indeed reduce the chances of finding remedies to them."*

1.2. Replicating the Grameen Model

The success of the program in Bangladesh prompted the Grameen Foundation to consider possible countries where the model could be replicated. Grameen Foundation USA and MTN Uganda launched an initiative to replicate the success of the Village Phone program in Uganda. The initiative has four goals:

1. To provide the rural communities of Uganda with valuable communications services to enable them to break the cycle of poverty;
2. To establish a general replication model;
3. To validate, measure, and document the model in a single country;
4. To disseminate this learning to the commercial telecommunications sector and the worldwide development communities to establish a global Village Phone movement.

In November 2003, MTN villagePhone (MTNVP) was formally created and launched as an independent company and "a sustainable initiative that aims to alleviate poverty and empower rural Ugandans through the provision of communications services". The total project goal is to establish 5000 new MTNVP micro-enterprises, which will only be possible by combining the reach of your microfinance institution with the largest mobile operator in Uganda. Over 50% of the population of Uganda is now covered by MTN mobile cellular

2.0 THE STRUCTURE OF THE BUSINESS

2.1 Roles and Responsibilities

There are five parties that are needed to make this program a success. The following graphic illustrates their roles and responsibilities;

Telecom Operator
- Provide and validate communications coverage to needed rural areas
- Source, stock and on-sell all equipment for Village Phone Company
- Sell prepaid airtime cards to MFIs
- Usage data to Village Phone Company
- Government licensing & regulation compliance
- Customer Care centre for VPOs
- Strategic planning with partners
- Allocate two board positions

The Catalyst Organization / Individual
- Ad hoc project management (for two years)
- Manage initial MFI enrolment and agreements
- Develop Operations Manual
- Develop VPO Manual and MFI Manual
- Allocate two board positions
- Strategic planning with partners

Village Phone Company
- Strategic planning, program monitoring & evaluation
- Relationship management with MFI partners
- Development of partner relationships for program expansion
- General problem solving
- Financial management
- Drive and plan network expansion
- Support of VPOs and MFIs
- Coordinate media and PR with *Telecom Operator*
- Training of MFI staff
- Knowledge consolidation and dissemination
- Usage reporting to MFIs
- Marketing

Microfinance Institution (MFI)
- Process VPO selection, applications & appointments
- Credit finance to VPO for purchase of phone & starter kits
- Conduit for equipment to VPOs
- Channel to market
- Conduit for airtime cards to VPOs
- Strategic planning with partners
- Customer support and problem solving for VPO
- Monitor appropriate use of phones and airtime
- Monitoring, evaluation and reporting of VPO performance

Village Phone Operator (VPO)
- Marketing of Village Phone business
- User billing and payment collection
- Airtime purchasing through MFI
- Providing communications service to the community using VP approved tariffs
- A communications knowledge resource to the community
- Equipment maintenance

2.2 Geographic Distribution

The goal of *Village Phone Company* is to provide communications access to as many poor rural *Country* as possible utilizing the Grameen shared access model. As such, the partnership model has been designed to ensure that there are open avenues to access these services for all microfinance institution members, regardless of their particular affiliation. Therefore, there can be no dedicated 'franchise areas' where a particular microfinance institution has sole rights to deploy phones. Rather, it is possible that within a particular district there will be more than one microfinance institution deploying phones amongst their membership.

The key element of success of the Grameen model is the business viability of each Village Phone Operator. One critical role that *Village Phone Company* assumes is buffering each Village Phone Operator from competition from another Village Phone Operator, giving each Village Phone Operator an opportunity to succeed. *Village Phone Company* will ensure that the zones of 'non-competition' will be respected within the family of Village Phone Operators.

Village Phone Company is not designed to meet the needs of the urban or peri-urban communities. The goal of the program is to provide communications services where no such viable, affordable, accessible alternatives exist – this is in the rural areas where the average villager must travel many kilometers to make a call and can pay very high rates. *Village Phone Company* phones will not be deployed in urban or peri-urban areas and the tariff rates are not designed to compete with the myriad of operators on the streets and booths of every urban center. They have been designed to provide affordable communications services to all rural people.

3.0 THE BUSINESS MODEL

3.1 Multiple Partners

There are multiple levels at which this business operates and all must be viable in their own right. There are no subsidies in this business model and each aspect of the overall system operates profitably and in a manner that is sustainable. Consider the model at the various levels:

Project Partner	Business Model	Sustainability Notes
Telecom Operator	Airtime sales yield profits on prior infrastructure investments	*Telecom Operator* is a for-profit corporate entity who wishes to reach a greater customer base in poor rural areas and who recognizes that they can do so profitably using a shared access model and utilizing the channel to market and financing infrastructure of microfinance networks.
MFI	Fee for service. In recognizing an opportunity cost for *Telecom Operator* in establishing a rural channel to market, the microfinance partner can share ongoing airtime revenues with *Telecom Operator*. The MFI gets a percentage of all airtime used by their network of Village Phone Operators. Additionally; the MFI reaps the benefit of the financing agreement with the Village Phone Operator from interest income.	Revenues to the microfinance partner are based on airtime usage. The marginal cost of delivery is small as they utilize their existing infrastructure to reach their constituency – the Village Phone Operators are their 'customers'
Village Phone Company	Revenue for this partner is derived from airtime sales and a revenue sharing model with the other partners.	Revenues cover the management and administration costs for the program.
Village Phone Operator	Sells airtime for outgoing calls. Market integrity and stability is maintained by ensuring that the phone is utilized only for its intended purpose – rural shared access mobile communications. Village Phones are fixed wireless public access phones, i.e. the location is fixed. Also generates revenue from non-airtime sources such as message delivery, solar charger utilization and so on.	Entrepreneurial driven business creates innovation in the marketplace. Competition is ensured through pricing strategies and is self limiting due to the rural nature of the targeted villages and the remoteness of the base station.

In Bangladesh, the lesson learned is that the model works because everyone is a 'winner'.

- The 'customer': who sees an immediate financial return (in terms of opportunity costs) and who gets a personalized 'delivery' service
- The Village Phone Operator: who is making a profit on the margin between their cost and the sale price for airtime and still providing a valuable service to the community.
- *Telecom Operator*: who now reach customers previously economically inaccessible at a small marginal cost and at a lower margin, but at a significantly greater volume yielding much greater revenue per phone than 'typical' urban subscribers.
- MFIs: who find value in the social yield but also in the ongoing revenue stream from credit agreements from Village Phone Operators and from the airtime sales which perpetuate themselves with little additional resources or input.
- *Village Phone Company* which covers its costs and generates a surplus in which to extend its mission driven expansion throughout Uganda.

4.0 VILLAGE PHONE HELP LINE

4.1 Types of Calls to Expect

Technical problems with equipment

Many Village Phone Operators who have no previous experience with mobile phones face challenges using their equipment. Customer service representatives must familiarize themselves with the equipment provided to Village Phone Operators as well as the many possible problems that can occur when operating this equipment in rural areas.

Broken Equipment

As the environment in rural areas can be very demanding on phone equipment and many Village Phone Operators are not accustomed to caring for this type of equipment, failure occurs. Customer service representatives should be prepared to answer a wide range of questions related to broken equipment. Anything from cows stepping on solar panels to "fried batteries" resulting from electrical surges in villages may occur to equipment. It is important to refer to the following information provided to Village Phone Operators and microfinance institutions to answer questions related to warranty and repair.

Problems Loading Airtime

Many Village Phone Operators who have no previous experience with mobile phones will have problems loading their airtime cards. Due to network congestion it is also common for the Telecom Operator platform supporting automated airtime loading to fail. Customer service representatives should be able to load airtime cards for Village Phone Operators when they experience these problems. An important part of being a Village Phone service representative is helping to educate Village Phone Operators on how to use their equipment. This empowers them to solve their own problems in the future and reduces repeated calls for the same problems.

Questions about Tariffs

Some Village Phone Operators who do not read English well may have trouble understanding the Village Phone Operator manual provided to them upon training. This can lead to a variety of questions including questions related to the tariffs they must charge with their business.

Battery Charging Problems

Village Phone Operators may experience problems charging their phones or battery failure problems due to charging the phone from an inappropriate source. It is important to refer to the information provided below for both warranty information as well as the solutions to common problems experienced when charging the phone.

4.2 Frequently Asked Questions, Common Problems & Solutions

Airtime

I have tried and failed to load an airtime card.

- Record the number of times the Village Phone Operator has attempted to load the airtime. Load the airtime for the Village Phone Operator and make sure they understand how to do it themselves.

Can I buy airtime cards in lower denominations?

- Document the request and tell them that they must speak to their respective microfinance group to address this question.

How do I check my airtime?

- *Code* will display the airtime and service fee on the phone. Dialing just *code* will give an automated voice response stating the airtime and service fee expiry date for the phone.

Phone

The phone heats up when charging,

- This could mean that the phone is defective or that they have misused the phone. Document the problem and report it to Village Phone staff.

The phone does not turn on.

- One must hold down the red button on the phone for a few seconds to turn it on. If this fails to work, it could be a battery problem or a defective phone. These problems are addressed in the following sections.

Why does my phone number not show up on the phone I call (beeping)?

- The caller identification feature has been disabled for Village Phones to give Village Phone Operators a business advantage. Village Phone Operators do not profit if people use their phone to beep friends and then have them call back. Explain to the Village Phone Operator that this is for the benefit of their Village Phone business.

My phone says it is locked. How do I unlock it?

- It is possible to accidentally enable the password / lock out feature on the phone. If this occurs the password to get back on, if they haven't changed it, is 0000. They just type in 0000 and then press OK and the phone should be activated.

I broke my phone. What do I do?

- Village Phone Operators are told when they receive their phones that they are responsible for proper care of their equipment. If something breaks due to their negligence this is their responsibility. It is important to document the problem and report it to Village Phone staff.

Someone has stolen my phone.

- Tell them to report this to the police. Refer to the previous explanation above.

How do I get a Village Phone for my sister, neighbor?

- Tell them to contact their microfinance institution and apply for a Village Phone.

I am unable to make international calls.

- Refer to the Village Phone Operator Manual for instructions on how to make international calls and how to use country codes.

How do I write an SMS?

- Refer to the Samsung R220 phone manual to explain how to write messages.

Solar Panel

The solar panel takes a long time to charge.

- The solar panel works best when there is direct sunlight. It does not store power and thus does not work at night or when there is insufficient light. The solar panel has two sides; the black side must face the sun in order to work. The solar panel can take anywhere from 2 – 10 hours to charge the phone depending on clouds, positioning in the sun etc.

I am having problems charging with the solar panel.

- Document the problem and refer to the section above for common problems.

The phone shows that the battery is charging, but when I take it off the solar panel the battery has been discharged.

- The car charger adapter could possibly be faulty or one of the connections from the solar panel to the phone. Document the problem and report to Village Phone staff.
- Use the car battery to charge the phone.

I broke my solar panel. What do I do?

- Village Phone Operators are told when they receive their phones that they are responsible for proper care of their equipment. If something breaks due to their negligence this is their responsibility. It is important to document the problem and report it to Village Phone staff.

Car Battery

My car battery is no longer charging the phone.

- This could mean that they need to take the car battery to town for charging at a battery service center. It is important for Village Phone Operators to charge the car battery before it is completely discharged, otherwise it may not work or may function ineffectively. We recommend to them to charge the car battery every two months to prevent the problem. If they have any doubts about when they last charged the car battery they should take it for charging.

I have spilled some of the battery acid out of the battery.

- The Village Phone Operator must take the battery to a local Authorized Service Center that services Telecom Operator phones to make sure that it is still functioning properly and have the battery acid refilled.

Antenna (Arial)

How do I adjust my antenna?

- Refer to the Village Phone Operator Manual regarding antenna installation and adjustment.

My antenna fell over and broke.

- Village Phone operators are told when they receive their phones that they are responsible for proper care of their equipment. If something breaks due to their negligence this is their responsibility. It is important to document the problem and report it to Village Phone staff.

Village Phone Business

Do I charge people for phone calls if the network cuts out?

- Yes. This is to their discretion but they must understand that they are paying for the customers call and if they do charge for the call, then they will be losing money.

Someone has stolen my signpost.

- If any Village Phone equipment is lost or stolen it is the responsibility of the Village Phone Operator. Document and report this information.

How much do I charge for international calls, SMS ... ?

- Refer to the tariffs section in the Village Phone Operator Manual.

5.0 VILLAGE PHONE CUSTOMER SERVICE RESPONSIBILITIES

As a Village Phone customer service representative you are on the front line dealing with the many challenges that Village Phone Operators experience. As Village Phone Company is a new and rapidly expanding business it is very important to document the types of calls, types of callers, problems and anomalies that are reported to you from Village Phone Operators. This information will be used to improve the product as well as adapt to changing service needs of Village Phone Operators.

For each call it is important to document the phone number of the caller, and the problem that they have experienced as well as any additional pertinent information that could help Village Phone Company in the future.

APPENDIX G: HEADS OF AGREEMENT TEMPLATE

Date

1.	DEFINITIONS	MFI – Micro Finance Institute VPO – Village Phone Operator
2.	BRANDING & ADVERTISING	How will the product be branded? Who will be responsible for advertising?
3.	DEPLOYMENT OUTREACH TARGET	What are the goals for the company? For example, the target deployment for village Phones into rural Uganda was 5,000, over five years.
4.	INSTITUTIONAL SUSTAINABILITY TARGET	At what point will the Village Phone company be able to cover its operational costs with revenues from airtime sales?
5.	PARTIES TO THIS AGREEMENT	What are the names of the partners?
6.	TERM OF AGREEMENT	How long will the agreement be in place?
7.	HARDWARE and EQUIPMENT	Who is responsible for procurement, packaging, and branding of all equipment? What will the total cost for the equipment package be? What equipment will be supplied to the VPOs? For example, in Uganda the equipment supplied to the VPO includes: ▪ A GSM handset ▪ An external Yagi antenna with suitable cable and connectors ▪ Automobile battery with cable and female cigarette lighter plug ▪ A GSM SIM card ▪ A 100,000 /= airtime card ▪ Marketing materials ▪ How will warranty issues be addressed? What margin, if any, will be added to equipment costs?
8.	AIRTIME CARD DISTRIBUTION	How will airtime be distributed to Village Phone Operators? Are there any constraints to how airtime will be sold?

continued

9.	AIRTIME	What will the charges for airtime be? Are there any additional service fees?
10.	PHONE SERVICING	How will phones be serviced if the Village Phone Operator has a problem? Who bears the cost?
11.	LOCATION	Where will Village Phones be located? Are there any constraints on where a Village Phone business can be placed? Can Village Phone Operators change location?
12.	ORGANIZATIONAL STRUCTURE	What is the structure of the new Village Phone company? What is the company's name? How many shares will be issued (and to whom)? How is the company capitalized? How many people serve on the board of directors? How are strategic decisions made? How will profits from operations be used or distributed? How frequently will board meetings take place?
13.	FINANCING	How will the company be capitalized? How much money will be required? How much is each party contributing? Are there limits to claims the funders can make on the company?
14.	PERFORMANCE BASED BUYOUT	Is there an option for one partner to buy-out the other partner? How is that price determined? Can shares be resold?
15.	DIVIDEND POLICY	When will dividends be paid? Is there a minimum amount that is paid? Will dividend payments have any impact on operations?
16.	STAFFING REQUIREMENTS	What are the staffing requirements for the company? What jobs need to be filled?
17.	USAGE REPORTING and ACCESS TO SYSTEMS	How are usage reports produced? To whom are reports distributed and at what frequency?
18.	USAGE TARGETS & ASSUMPTIONS	What assumptions are being made in the business model for: ■ number of minutes sold per phone per day ■ deployment targets for goals ■ tariffs and margins for all parties
19.	REVENUE SHARING	How is revenue split between each party?
20.	GOVERNMENT LICENSING	Who is responsible for addressing all government licensing and regulation compliance issues?
21.	GOVERNMENT TAXATION	Who will be responsible for the payment of necessary VAT and other relevant taxes?

continued

22.	CUSTOMER SUPPORT	Who is responsible for on-air support to Village Phone Operators? When will support be available?
23.	RECRUITING	Who is responsible for recruiting and hiring staff?
24.	PILOT PROJECT	What is the timing of the pilot project? What are the goals, objectives, and decision points for the pilot?
25.	FORMAL LAUNCH AND ROLLOUT	When will the Village Phone Company and Program be formally announced?
26.	MEDIA LAUNCH	When will a media launch occur for the Village Phone Company?
27.	FINANCIAL MANAGEMENT	What is the revenue receipt policy (e.g., 45 days)?
28.	INTELLECTUAL PROPERTY	Who owns the intellectual property which is created as part of the daily operations of the Village Phone Company?

APPENDIX H: EQUIPMENT SUPPLIERS

Yagi Antennas and Cables

The antenna solution for Uganda and Rwanda was sourced from:

> Skymasts Antennas Ltd
> Equilibrium House
> Mansion Close
> Moulton Park Industrial Estate
> Northampton
> NN3 6RU, England
> +44(0) 1604 494132
> carl.jones@skymasts.com

Tariff boards

Signs for Uganda and Rwanda were produced by Precision Signz:

> http://www.precisionsignz.com
> 1055 Valley Dr
> Bettendorf, IA 52722
> Phone 563-441-4444 or 866-744-6778
> Fax 563-441-2222
> salessignz@precisionsignz.com

Battery Cables

The cables used to attach the automobile battery to the cigarette charger adapter for Uganda and Rwanda was sourced from:

> UltraTec
> Abhay Shah
> Kampala, Uganda
> ultratecug@usa.net

Mobile Phone Service

In Uganda and Rwanda, repair of mobile phones is handled by Cellular Service Logistics:

> http://www.cslafrica.com/

APPENDIX I: SAMPLE BUSINESS MODEL

SAMPLE INCOME STATEMENT

	Yr1	Yr2	Yr3	Yr4	Yr5
Revenue	-	-	-	-	-
Call revenue	-	-	-	-	-
Operational costs	-	-	-	-	-
Salaries	-	-	-	-	-
Manager	-	-	-	-	-
Admin assistant	-	-	-	-	-
Field Officers	-	-	-	-	-
Training for staff	-	-	-		-
Automobile expenses (fuel, tires, insurance, maintenance)		-			-
Various equipment (computers, phones)	-	-	-		-
Office rent, electricity, water	-	-	-		-
External consultant fees	-	-		-	-
External audit	-	-	-		-
Marketing	-	-	-		-
Outsourced support services (Accounting, Human Resrouces, Legal, Procurement, Vehicle maintenance Customer support, IT and Reporting)	-	-	-		-
Domestic travel and communications for staff	-	-	-	-	-
EBITDA	-	-	-	-	-
Depreciation	-	-	-	-	-
Profit/(Loss) before finance charges	-	-	-		-
Financial costs	-	-	-	-	-
Loan interests	-	-	-	-	-
Profit/(Loss) before Tax	-	-	-	-	-
Less Taxes	-	-	-	-	-
Corporation Tax	-	-	-	-	-
Profit/(Loss) after Tax	-	-	-	-	-
Accumulated Profit/(Loss) from previous period	-	-		-	
Retained Earnings/(Accum. Loss)	-	-	-	-	-

SAMPLE BALANCE SHEET

	Yr1	Yr2	Yr3	Yr4	Yr5
ASSETS					
Non Current Assets	-	-	-	-	-
Fixed asset cost	-	-	-	-	-
Depreciation	-	-	-	-	-
Current Assets	-	-	-	-	-
Cash and deposits	-	-	-	-	-
Accounts receivable	-	-	-	-	-
Total Assets	-	-	-	-	-
EQUITY & LIABILITIES					
Equity	-	-	-	-	-
Share Capital	-	-	-	-	-
Accumulated Profits/(Losses)	-	-	-	-	-
Liabilities	-	-	-	-	-
Long term borrowings	-	-	-	-	-
Interest on long term loans	-	-	-	-	-
Total Equity & Liabilities	-	-	-	-	-

SAMPLE CASH FLOW STATEMENT

	Yr1	Yr2	Yr3	Yr4	Yr5
Cash Flow from Operating Activities	-	-	-	-	-
Other operational cash flows	-	-	-	-	-
Depreciation	-	-	-	-	-
Interest expense	-	-	-	-	-
Net Cash Flows from Operating Activities	-	-	-	-	-
Net Cash Flows from Investing Activities	-	-	-	-	-
(Purchase)/Disposal of assets	-	-	-	-	-
Net cash flows before funding requirements/commitments	-	-	-	-	-
Net Cash Flows from Funding Activities	-	-	-	-	-
Injection of Share Capital		-	-	-	-
Proceeds from Long Term Loan	-		-	-	-
In-kind long term loans					
Repayment of Long Term loan		-	-		-
Payment of Loan Interest		-	-	-	-
Net Cash & Cash Equivalents for period	-	-	-	-	-
Cash & Cash Equivalents at beginning of period	-	-	-	-	-
Cash & Cash Equivalents at end of period	0	0	0	0	0

SAMPLE REVENUE

	Jan-03	Feb-03	Mar-03	Apr-03
Month	1	2	3	4
Opening Base	-	-	-	-
Net additions	-	-	-	-
Closing Base	-	-	-	-
Average Base	-	-	-	-
Usage Assumptions				
Billable Minutes per Month	-	-	-	-
Retail Tariff to end users (Including VAT)	-	-	-	-
Wholesale Tariff to VPOs (Incl. VAT)	-	-	-	-
Discount for distribution channel (MFI)	-	-	-	-
Revenue to Telecommunications Company (Incl. VAT)	-	-	-	-
Revenue to Telecommunications Company (Excl. VAT)	-	-	-	-
(VPO) Retail Margin per Billable Minute	-	-	-	-
Total Retail Revenues	-	-	-	-
Revenues to TelCo and Village Phone Company	-	-	-	-
Less any special discount program for VPOs	-	-	-	-
Actual Retail Revenues	0	0	0	0
Share Of Wholesale Revenues				
Telecommunications Company	0.0%	0.0%	0.0%	0.0%
Village Phone Company	0.0%	0.0%	0.0%	0.0%
Total	0%	0%	0%	0%
Revenues to Respective Parties				
Telecommunications Company	-	-	-	-
Village Phone Company	-	-	-	-
Cumulative Revenues to Respective Parties				
Telecommunications Company	-	-	-	-
Village Phone Company	-	-	-	-

TRAFFIC SENSITIVITY

Month	Jan-03	Feb-03	Mar-03	Apr-03	May-03	Jun-03
Month days	31	28	31	30	31	30
Period	5	6	7	8	9	10
Operational Period	1	2	3	4	5	6
Min Use per day	0	0	0	0	0	0
Min Use per month	0	0	0	0	0	0
Phones Installed this month	0	0	0	0	0	0
Cumulative Phones	0	0	0	0	0	0
Active rate	100%	100%	100%	100%	100%	100%
Billable Minutes per month	0	0	0	0	0	0

SAMPLE TARIFF STRUCTURE

	Retail Price Per Min	Cost per min to VPO
•Local calls	-	-
•Regional calls	-	-
•Rest of the World	-	-
•Other carriers	-	-
•SMS	-	-
•International SMS	-	-

Traffic Mix

Local calls	Regional calls	Rest of the World	Other carriers	Total
0.0%	0%	0.0%	0%	0.0%

Tariffs to increase in yr 3-4 by	0%
Tariffs to increase in yr 5 by	0%

	Yr 1-2	Yr 3-4	Yr 5
Avg retail tariff (including VAT)	-	0.00	0.00
Avg wholesale tariff to VPOs	0.00	0.00	0.00

SAMPLE PAYROLL AND STAFFING

Designation	Y1	Y2	Y3	Y4	Y5
Manager	-	-	-	-	-
Admin assistant	-	-	-	-	-
Field Officers	-	-	-	-	-
# of Field Officers	1	2	2	2	2
Total staff	3	4	4	4	4

ONLINE MODEL AVAILABLE

A more detailed version of the Sample Business Model (with additional sheets and calculations that populate data in the above financial statements) is available electronically from http://www.gfusa.org/technology center/ and other websites from where this Replication Manual can be downloaded .